CENTRAL OREGON
CASCADE LAKES
Scenic Drive & Recreation
GUIDE

Produced by
Sun Publishing

716 NE 4th St. • Bend, OR 97701 • (541) 382-0127 • Fax: (541) 382-7057 • www.sun-pub.com • sunpub@sun-pub.com

PERSONNEL: Geoff Hill – Publisher/Editor • Vicki Hill – Financial Manager • Jan Siegrist – Editor/Graphic Design/Production

ABOVE: A backpacker enjoys the view below Broken Top. ©Fred Pflughoft/Gnass Photo Images
ON THE COVER: South Sister dominates the view from this stretch of the Cascade Lakes Highway. ©Jon Gnass/Gnass Photo Images
INSIDE FRONT COVER: The highway offers several pull-off spots for photo opportunities such as this one featuring Broken Top. Photo by Geoff Hill

Boat dock at Lava Lake with Broken Top, Broken Hand, and Ball Butte in the distance. Photo by Geoff Hill

From high desert to high lakes and high mountains, the Cascade Lakes region offers visitors an incredibly beautiful area in which to play and explore.

The Cascade Lakes Highway (Oregon State Highway 46) became a National Scenic Byway in 1998. National Scenic Byways must possess one or more of six intrinsic qualities: natural, scenic, recreational, archaeological, cultural, or historic. The Cascade Lakes Highway is noted for its scenic, natural, and recreational qualities.

This book will be useful as a drive and tour guide for visitors as well as a souvenir "picture" book.

The Cascade Lakes Scenic Drive locator map on page 14 has corresponding pages with detailed descriptions and symbols indicating the recreational opportunities and amenities available at each specific location.

We hope that the beautiful photos and descriptive words in this scenic guide will entice you to explore this area on your own ... and discover for yourself its splendor.

PHOTOS (from top):
Rafting the Deschutes River. Photo courtesy of Sun Country Tours
Strolling in Drake Park in downtown Bend. Photo by Scott Schechtel
Riding the sightseeing chairlift at Mt. Bachelor. Photo courtesy of Mt. Bachelor
Camping at Devils Lake. Photo by Bob Woodward

BEST BETS FOR
Having Fun

Below are our "best bets" as to where you can go for the following activities and amenities; however, these activities are not limited to the areas listed below.

In this book, you will find detailed descriptions of all of these areas and others, and you may discover that your own "best bet" differs from ours!

This key corresponds with the symbols in the corresponding editorial information. See the locator map and key on page 14 and 15.

BIKING: Swampy Lakes • Mt. Bachelor • Cultus Lake

BOATING: Sparks Lake • Elk Lake • Cultus Lake • Wickiup Reservoir

CAMERA OPPORTUNITIES: Everywhere!

CAMPING: Elk, Lava, Cultus, and Twin lakes; Crane Prairie and Wickiup Reservoirs

CANOEING & KAYAKING: Sparks Lake • Hosmer Lake • Little Lava Lake
Little Cultus Lake • North and South Twin lakes • Deschutes River

FISHING: Hosmer (fly fishing) • Lava and Twin lakes • Crane Prairie Reservoir, Wickiup Reservoir • Deschutes and Fall rivers

GAS AVAILABLE: Elk Lake • Cultus Lake • Crane Prairie Reservoir • South Twin Lake

GROCERIES: Elk Lake • Cultus Lake • Lava Lake • Crane Prairie Reservoir • South Twin Lake

HIKING: Tumalo Mountain • Sparks Lake area
Green Lakes, Six Lakes and Lucky Lakes Trailheads • Cultus Mountain

HORSEBACK RIDING: Todd Lake • Quinn Meadow Horse Camp

MOTOR BOATING: Elk Lake • Lava Lake • Cultus Lake • Crane Prairie and Wickiup Reservoirs

PICNICKING: Drake Park • Mt. Bachelor • Todd, Elk, Lava, and Twin Lakes
Lava Lands Visitor Center

RESORTS: Elk Lake • Cultus Lake • Crane Prairie Reservoir • South Twin Lake

RESTAURANTS: Mt. Bachelor • Elk Lake • Cultus Lake • South Twin Lake

RV FACILITIES: Elk Lake • Lava Lake • Cultus Lake • Crane Prairie Reservoir • South Twin Lak

SAILING & WINDSURFING: Elk Lake • Cultus Lake • Wickiup Reservoir

SWIMMING: Elk Lake • Lava Lakes • Cultus Lakes • Twin Lakes • Wickiup Reservoir

WATERSKIING: Cultus Lake • Wickiup Reservoir

AND FURTHERMORE:
DAY TRIP: The High Desert Museum
GEOLOGICAL ATTRACTIONS: Lava Cast Forest, Lava River Caves, Lava Lands Visitor Center

Contents

PHOTOS (from top):
Todd Lake. Photo by Brian O'Keefe; Horseback riding near The Inn of the Seventh Mountain. Courtesy of River Ridge Stables; An alpine vista below North and Middle Sisters. ©Jon Gnass/Gnass Photo Images.

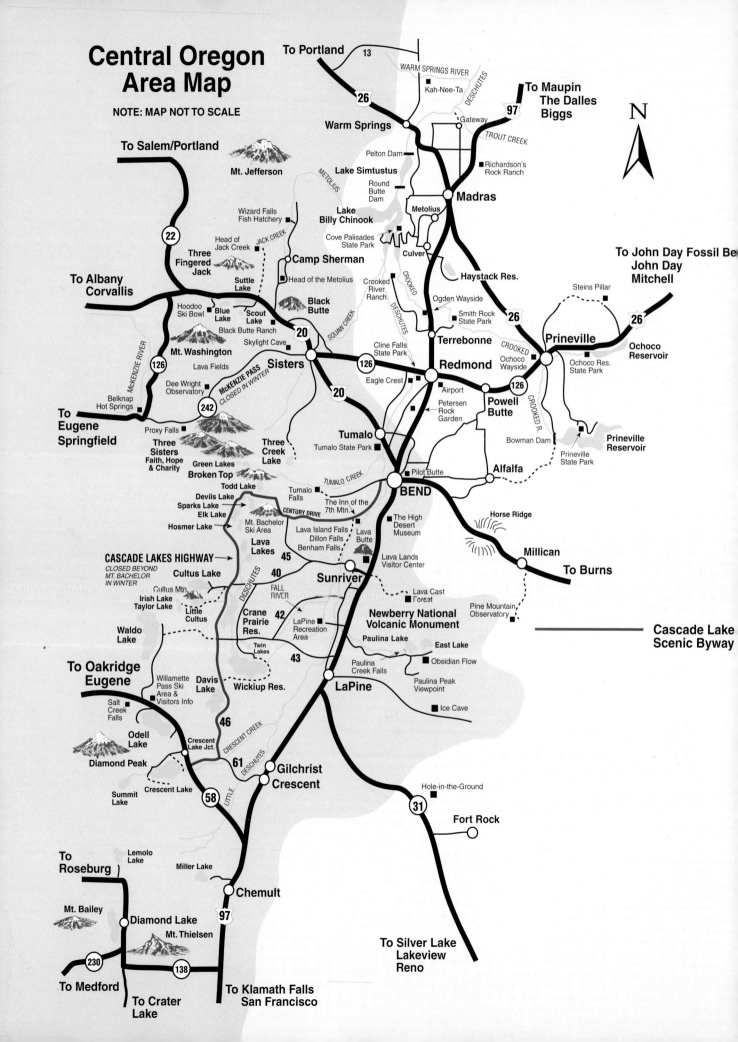

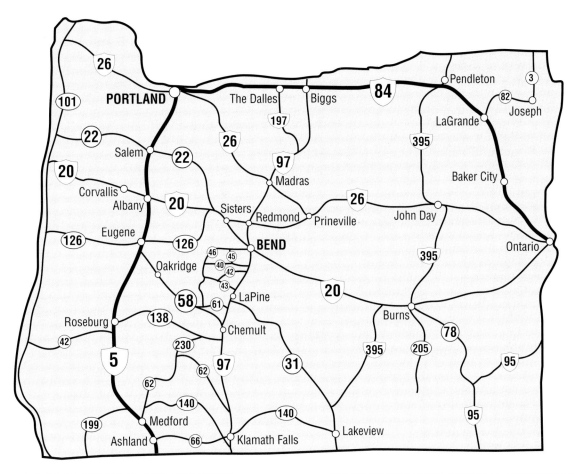

MILEAGE CHART TO OREGON CITIES

Bend to:	Miles	Bend to:	Miles
Albany	105	Klamath Falls	135
Ashland	201	LaGrande	236
Astoria	260	Lakeview	176
Baker City	198	LaPine	30
Black Butte Ranch	28	Madras	45
Burns	131	McMinnville	155
Camp Sherman	35	Medford	178
Chemult	65	Newport	192
Coos Bay	208	Oakridge	115
Corvallis	116	Ontario	262
Crescent	45	Pendleton	265
Crooked River Ranch	30	Portland	156
Eagle Crest Resort	13	Prineville	35
Eugene	121	Redmond	16
Gilchrist	44	Salem	130
Grants Pass	184	Seaside	238
Hood River	153	Sisters	20
The Inn of the Seventh		Sunriver	15
Mountain Resort	6	The Dalles	133
Kah-Nee-Ta Resort	70		

MILEAGE CHART TO CENTRAL OREGON LAKES

Bend to:	Miles	Bend to:	Miles
Crane Prairie Reservoir	45	Lava Lake	41
Crater Lake	119	Little Lava Lake	41
Crescent Lake	76	Miller Lake	72
Cultus Lake	48	Ochoco Reservoir	40
Little Cultus Lake	50	Odell Lake	79
Davis Lake	58	Paulina Lake	33
Devils Lake	29	Prineville Reservoir	50
Diamond Lake	90	Sparks Lake	30
East Lake	38	Suttle Lake	35
Elk Lake	33	Three Creek Lake	40
Green Lakes	33	Todd Lake	27
Haystack Reservoir	32	North Twin Lake	42
Hosmer Lake	39	South Twin Lake	44
Lake Billy Chinook	40	Wickiup Reservoir	45
Lake Simtustus	53	*Note: Mileages are approximate*	

CASCADE MOUNTAIN IDENTIFIER

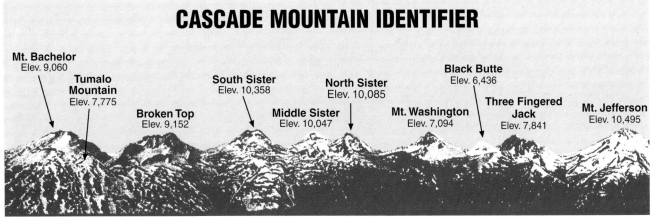

Identifier courtesy of First American Title Insurance Company of Oregon

A GRAND TOUR of the CASCADE LAKES HIGHWAY

A One-Day Driving Tour of the Cascade Lakes Highway

The following is a one-day driving tour of the Cascade Lakes Highway with stops at many of the lakes along the way. As this tour is intended to be done in one full day, the information in the following article is an overview of the highlights along the highway. For further details on the amenities and activities of a specific area, refer to the related articles on individual areas on the following pages. In 1998, a lengthy section of this highway/tour was recognized as a National Scenic Byway.

By George W. Linn

QUESTION. WHAT IS THE CASCADE LAKES HIGHWAY?
There is no single answer to that question, because every person has his or her own way of answering it. Ask it of a hundred different people, and you're likely to get a hundred different answers. And each is correct.

It's Oregon's most scenic drive.

Best trout fishing in the state.

It's the best place to see the mountains close-up.

It takes you to Mt. Bachelor and that great powder snow.

It's so unspoiled.

You can see more lakes and beautiful lakes on this highway than you can on any other highway in the state — or maybe even the world.

It's snowmobile country.

It's the jump-off point for some of the nations' best hiking and backpacking trails.

The air is so clean.

It gets you right to the edge of the wilderness area.

I feel so close to God.

It has everything — mountains, pines, lakes — you name it.

TOP: The Cascade Lakes Highway is the jump-off point for some of the nations' best hiking and backpacking trails, all offering a wide variety of scenery and incredible views. Photo by Don Burgderfer

BOTTOM: South Sister and fog reflect in Sparks Lake on a morning in July. © Jon Gnass / Gnass Photo Images

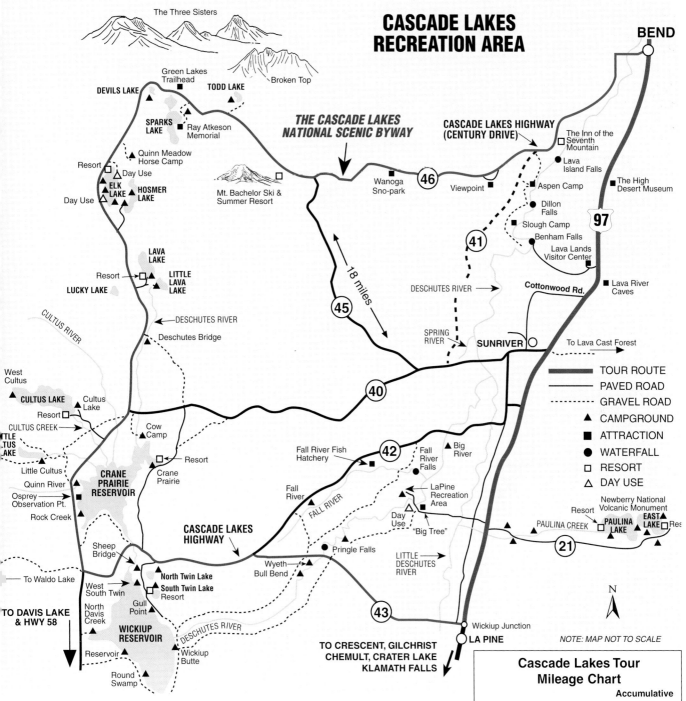

CASCADE LAKES RECREATION AREA

The Three Sisters

Broken Top

Green Lakes Trailhead

DEVILS LAKE

TODD LAKE

SPARKS LAKE

Ray Atkeson Memorial

Quinn Meadow Horse Camp

Resort

Day Use

ELK LAKE

HOSMER LAKE

Day Use

THE CASCADE LAKES NATIONAL SCENIC BYWAY

Mt. Bachelor Ski & Summer Resort

Wanoga Sno-park

Viewpoint

CASCADE LAKES HIGHWAY (CENTURY DRIVE)

The Inn of the Seventh Mountain

Lava Island Falls

Aspen Camp

The High Desert Museum

46

41

97

Dillon Falls

Slough Camp

Benham Falls

Lava Lands Visitor Center

DESCHUTES RIVER

Cottonwood Rd.

Lava River Caves

LAVA LAKE

Resort

LITTLE LAVA LAKE

LUCKY LAKE

18 miles

45

DESCHUTES RIVER

Deschutes Bridge

CULTUS RIVER

West Cultus

CULTUS LAKE

Cultus Lake

Resort

CULTUS CREEK

TLE TUS AKE

Little Cultus

Quinn River

Osprey Observation Pt.

Rock Creek

CRANE PRAIRIE RESERVOIR

Cow Camp

Resort

Crane Prairie

40

SPRING RIVER

SUNRIVER

To Lava Cast Forest

TOUR ROUTE
PAVED ROAD
GRAVEL ROAD
▲ CAMPGROUND
■ ATTRACTION
● WATERFALL
□ RESORT
△ DAY USE

Fall River Fish Hatchery

42

Fall River Falls

Big River

CASCADE LAKES HIGHWAY

Fall River

FALL RIVER

LaPine Recreation Area

Day Use

"Big Tree"

Newberry National Volcanic Monument

Resort

PAULINA LAKE

EAST LAKE

Res

PAULINA CREEK

21

Sheep Bridge

To Waldo Lake

West South Twin

North Twin Lake

South Twin Lake Resort

Gull Point

North Davis Creek

WICKIUP RESERVOIR

DESCHUTES RIVER

Pringle Falls

Wyeth Bull Bend

LITTLE DESCHUTES RIVER

TO DAVIS LAKE & HWY 58

Reservoir

Wickiup Butte

Round Swamp

Wickiup Junction

LA PINE

TO CRESCENT, GILCHRIST CHEMULT, CRATER LAKE KLAMATH FALLS

N

NOTE: MAP NOT TO SCALE

43

See what I mean? Each person sees it in a different light. As one famous poet put it: "Beauty is in the eye of the beholder." So it is with the Cascade Lakes Highway — also known as Century Drive or, less romantically, Oregon State Highway 46. For our "Grand Tour of the Cascade Lakes Highway," let's stick with that name; however, I will point out that you will see signs on the trip identifying it all three ways, as well as an Oregon Scenic Byway.

If you would like a more detailed map of the Cascade Lakes area, stop at the Forest Service office in Bend on U.S. Highway 20 or in Red Oaks Square on Third Street and pick up a map of the Deschutes National Forest." It's the best investment you'll ever make if you plan to visit this area again and again.

So you have your map and this guidebook. You have at least

Cascade Lakes Tour Mileage Chart

	Accumulative Mileage
Bend (3rd St. & Franklin Ave.)	Start
Wanoga Sno-park	15.5
Mt. Bachelor Ski Area	23.3
Todd Lake Turn-off	25.3
Sparks Lake Boat Ramp	29.9
Devils Lake	32.9
Elk Lake	37.8
Lava Lake	45.6
Little Lava Lake	46.5
Cultus Lake	57.1

Mileage does not include side trips to Crane Prairie, Wickiup, and Twin Lakes

Fall River Junction	82.5
Wickiup Junction (U.S. 97)	93.1
Paulina Lake Turn-off	96.6
Bend (3rd St. & Franklin Ave.)	119.4

There is no single answer as to
"What is the Cascade Lakes Highway?"
One of Oregon's most scenic drives offers something for everyone
from fishing to boating, from hiking to camping,
from picnicking to relaxing and enjoying the drive!

From the deck at Mt. Bachelor's Pine Marten Lodge, the view of the surrounding mountains and Cascade lakes
is impressive. If you prefer not to hike up to see the view, Mt. Bachelor Ski Area offers summer sightseeing lift rides.
Photo by Bob Woodward courtesy of Mt. Bachelor

twice as much color film or digital camera disks as you think you could possible use? You've allowed the better part of the whole day for the trip? Then let's go!

OUR TOUR BEGINS AT THIRD STREET AND FRANKLIN AVENUE. Turn west onto Franklin and skirt the edge of Bend's downtown area. The route is well marked, and you should have no trouble following it through town. The climb begins immediately. By the time you reach The Inn of the Seventh Mountain, you will have climbed 700 feet. In the next seven miles, you will have climbed an additional 1,000 feet, and you will be over a mile high for the next 20 miles or so.

The closer you get to Mt. Bachelor, the more impressive it becomes. From a distance, this perfect example of a dormant volcano appears to be dwarfed by the Three Sisters; but it's only about 1,300 feet lower in elevation than the South Sister, the highest of the three. The highway brings you right to the base of the mountain.

Just before you get to the second Mt. Bachelor

turn-off, you receive one of the trip's most pleasant surprises. Suddenly, as you round a bend in the highway, there is a panoramic view of the Three Sisters and Broken Top directly in front of you — at close range. It reminds one of the Swiss Alps, an impregnable barrier of volcanic peaks with glaciers gracing their sides. Perhaps the highway engineer was a photographer, because there are several convenient turn-outs where one can get magnificent shots of this impressive array of mountain scenery. This view will be one of the trip's highlights.

Take time to drive into the Mt. Bachelor parking area nestled at the base of the symmetrical 9,000-foot cone. While the large parking lot may seem somewhat deserted or nearly so in mid-summer, it is filled to overflowing in mid-winter; because, the dry powder snow for which it is famous attracts skiers and snowboarders from an ever-widening circle. Skiing conditions at Mt. Bachelor are as fine as one will find anywhere in the nation, if not the world.

Within a couple of miles west of Mt. Bachelor is the

turn-off to Todd Lake, a beautiful alpine lake resplendent with wildflowers, sitting near the base of rugged Broken Top. This lake is often still snowbound in late June so check with the Forest Service for information. If accessible, it is a one-quarter mile hike to the lake from the parking area.

SPARKS LAKE IS OUR NEXT STOP.

In many ways, Sparks Lake is the most unique body of water on the Cascade Lakes Highway. The Forest Service sign identifies it as a "meadow lake," and that term seems appropriate. If it were not for the numerous creeks carrying the run-off from snow fields high on the sides of nearby mountains, it would be simply a meadow. The surrounding terrain is relatively flat. Trees and marshy grasses extend well out into the body of the lake. Many small islands and peninsulas break the water's surface. And, of all the major lakes on the Cascade Lakes Highway, it is the closest to the South Sister and Broken Top, making it especially scenic and photogenic.

The drive down the lake's east side to the Sparks Lake boat ramp is especially worthwhile. The cinder road is well maintained, and the view (especially if you're a photographer) is worth the drive. The lake was a favorite spot for famous Oregon photographer Ray Atkeson, and a trail bearing his name is located here.

Two well-known hiking trails leave the highway from the Sparks Lake area. One goes northeast along Soda Creek and approaches Todd Lake from the north. The other takes off from the Fall Creek bridge to Green Lakes directly between Broken Top and the Lewis Glacier on the eastern slope of the South Sister.

THE SMALLEST LAKE OF THE TOUR IS OUR NEXT STOP — DEVILS LAKE. The highway skirts its shores before turning southward on the second leg of the tour. From this point on there is a gradual drop in elevation.

Elk Lake is almost directly south of the South Sister and almost directly west of Mt. Bachelor. Consequently, it is almost impossible to photograph the lake without one of the two peaks in perfect position. The

Broken Top rises above Todd Lake in this view shot from the picnic area near Todd Creek. Photo by Don Burgderfer

INSET: The Forest Service provides informative, identifier signs at most of the high lakes. Photo by Geoff Hill

A windsurfer enjoys some solitude on Sparks Lake. South Sister dominates the background. Photo by Don Burgderfer

water is deep blue. Elk Lake Lodge sits on the the lake's western shore, facing Mt. Bachelor. A boat dock and launching ramp is here for the convenience of boaters and fishermen. The lodge offers a small, rustic restaurant and store.

Continuing southward, the highway hugs the lake's west shore, giving you innumerable vantage points. One of the most photogenic spots on Elk Lake is from the Beach Picnic Area at the lake's southernmost tip. Here, you have the full length of Elk Lake before you with the South Sister, Broken Top, and Mt. Bachelor in the background.

Dominating the skyline from both Lava Lake and Little Lava Lake is Mt. Bachelor. The lodge sits on the

the southern end of Lava Lake providing boat docks and a small store.

Little Lava Lake is especially interesting because the Deschutes River begins its winding course through Central Oregon from this small lake.

THE HIGHWAY FOLLOWS THE RIVER'S COURSE FOR SEVERAL MILES BEFORE IT TURNS WESTWARD TOWARD CULTUS LAKE, OUR NEXT STOP. The river is especially beautiful along this route as it meanders in and out of the pines and provides sustenance to the many green, grassy spots along its banks.

If we exclude Crane Prairie and Wickiup reservoirs, both of which are man-made lakes, Cultus Lake is the largest body of water on the Cascade Lakes Highway.

For some reason that is difficult to define, Cultus Lake has a different appearance than the other lakes visited on this tour. Perhaps it is because you approach the lake from the eastern end and have the full length stretched out before you, giving the appearance of an even larger body of water. Perhaps it's because, from the east end of the lake, there are no mountains in the background, and the emphasis is on the lake instead of the mountains. In any event,

ABOVE: Just past the entrance to Elk Lake Resort, a pull-off along the highway delivers a great view of the Cascade mountains and Elk Lake.

RIGHT: Colorful stream-side wildflowers can be seen along the highway.

FAR RIGHT: The boat dock at Lava Lake Resort is a great place to take in the view.

Photos by Geoff Hill

OSPREY SANCTUARY

Crane Prairie Reservoir Osprey Management Area is a cooperative venture by the U.S. Forest Service, Bureau of Reclamation and Oregon State Game Commission to provide the Osprey, a potentially endangered species, a safe place to live and propagate.
The management area is dedicated to the protection of the Osprey and its habitat.

• **U.S. DEPARTMENT OF AGRICULTURE** •

LEFT: Nesting osprey are a common sight at Crane Prairie. Photo by Brian O'Keefe

INSET: An osprey sanctuary is located on the west side of the reservoir, where a short path leads to a viewpoint. Photo by Don Burgderfer

BELOW: From the patio at Cultus Lake Resort, there is a nice view of the sandy beach along the lake. Photo by Geoff Hill

Cultus is a beautiful lake, offering the boater and the fisherman a great amount of open water.

The drive from Cultus to Little Cultus Lake is only about five miles, but it's a rough five miles. Of all the lakes on our tour, it is probably more in its natural state than any other, primarily because of its isolation. It is definitely worth seeing, so don't let my comments about the rough road scare you off. It is rough, but passable if you take it easy, even in a passenger car. There are few spots in Central Oregon which are accessible by car and as unspoiled by man.

From the two Cultus lakes, you continue southward, skirting the west side of Crane Prairie Reservoir. To continue on our tour of the Cascade Lakes Highway, you will follow the signs for the Highway, turning left as the road heads back to Highway 97. This section will take you between Crane Prairie and Wickiup reservoirs and past a turn-off for the Twin lakes. If you stay on this road, which bears right towards Pringle Falls (called Forest Service Road 43 here), you will come out on U.S. 97 at Wickiup Junction where you head north for your return trip to Bend. *(See page 62 for "Jewels of the Central Cascades," a tour of Crane Prairie, North and South Twin Lakes, and Wickiup Reservoir, as well as offering an alternate route back to Bend.)* If time allows, you might consider adding these side trips to today's tour.

The alternate route back to Bend is by way of Fall River. Instead of bearing right towards Pringle Falls on the FS Road 43, stay straight on FS Road 42, an all-paved route past the historic Vandevert Ranch to Sunriver and Highway 97.

Once you have made the "Grand Tour of the Cascade Lakes Highway," you will relive it many times; and, chances are, you will make the tour again and again. It's that kind of trip.

You will most certainly add your own definition of the Cascade Lakes Highway to the list at the beginning of this article. And, to you, your definition will be the only one that matters; because the tour is an emotional experience as well as a sight-seeing trip. ■

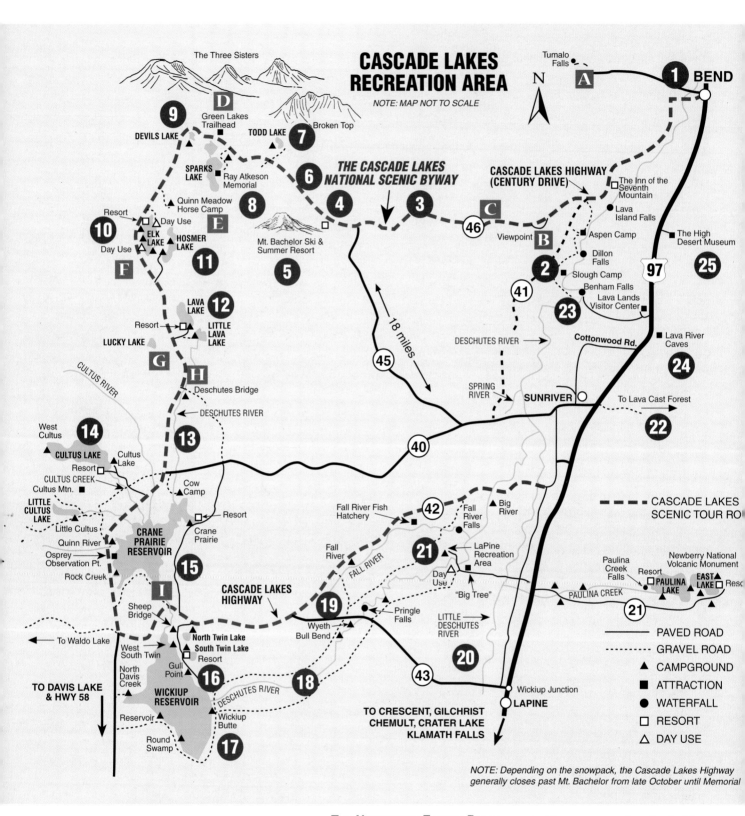

CASCADE LAKES RECREATION AREA

NOTE: MAP NOT TO SCALE

The Three Sisters

Tumalo Falls

A

1 BEND

9

Green Lakes Trailhead

DEVILS LAKE

D

Broken Top

TODD LAKE

7

THE CASCADE LAKES NATIONAL SCENIC BYWAY

CASCADE LAKES HIGHWAY (CENTURY DRIVE)

The Inn of the Seventh Mountain

SPARKS LAKE

Ray Atkeson Memorial

6

4

3

C

Lava Island Falls

Aspen Camp

The High Desert Museum

Quinn Meadow Horse Camp

8

46

Viewpoint

B

Dillon Falls

Resort

Day Use

E

10

ELK LAKE

HOSMER LAKE

25

Day Use

11

Mt. Bachelor Ski & Summer Resort

5

Slough Camp

97

F

2

41

Benham Falls

Lava Lands Visitor Center

23

LAVA LAKE

12

Resort

LITTLE LAVA LAKE

DESCHUTES RIVER

Cottonwood Rd.

Lava River Caves

LUCKY LAKE

G

18 miles

24

45

SPRING RIVER

H

Deschutes Bridge

CULTUS RIVER

DESCHUTES RIVER

SUNRIVER

To Lava Cast Forest

West Cultus

14

13

22

CULTUS LAKE

Cultus Lake

40

Resort

CULTUS CREEK

Cultus Mtn.

Cow Camp

Fall River Fish Hatchery

42

Big River

LITTLE CULTUS LAKE

Resort

Fall River Falls

CASCADE LAKES SCENIC TOUR RO

Little Cultus

Crane Prairie

21

LaPine Recreation Area

Paulina Creek Falls

Resort

Newberry National Volcanic Monument

Quinn River

CRANE PRAIRIE RESERVOIR

Fall River

Day Use

PAULINA LAKE

EAST LAKE Reso

Osprey Observation Pt.

15

FALL RIVER

"Big Tree"

PAULINA CREEK

Rock Creek

CASCADE LAKES HIGHWAY

19

Pringle Falls

21

I

Wyeth

LITTLE DESCHUTES RIVER

Sheep Bridge

Bull Bend

To Waldo Lake

North Twin Lake

South Twin Lake

20

— PAVED ROAD

West South Twin

Resort

- - - GRAVEL ROAD

▲ CAMPGROUND

North Davis Creek

Gull Point

16

18

43

Wickiup Junction

■ ATTRACTION

TO DAVIS LAKE & HWY 58

DESCHUTES RIVER

LAPINE

● WATERFALL

Reservoir

WICKIUP RESERVOIR

Wickiup Butte

TO CRESCENT, GILCHRIST CHEMULT, CRATER LAKE KLAMATH FALLS

□ RESORT

Round Swamp

17

△ DAY USE

NOTE: Depending on the snowpack, the Cascade Lakes Highway generally closes past Mt. Bachelor from late October until Memorial

---

NORTHWEST FOREST PASS

PASS ON YOUR NATURAL LEGACY

THE NORTHWEST FOREST PASS is required for many recreation sites in 16 national forests in Oregon and Washington. The Deschutes National Forest is part of the recreation fee program. Pass revenues provide a broad range of support to many facets of recreation including trail maintenance, cleaning and stocking comfort facilities, producing recreation guides, and interpretive centers.

Two passes are available: one-day and annual. Passes can be purchased at Deschutes National Forest offices, self-service locations, and local vendors throughout Central Oregon. They are also available online at www.fs.fed.us or by calling toll-free 1-800-270-7504.

NOTE: This Pass system is subject to change.

USING THE LOCATOR MAP

The page numbers below refer to the location in this book for each of the scenic areas along the tour route. Choose the location you would like to learn about and refer to the related page for further information on the activities and amenities available. The "Having Fun" symbols correspond with the editorial information.

LOCATOR MAP KEY

Northwest Forest Pass required

** Northwest Forest Pass required at trailheads in surrounding areas*

OTHER POINTS OF INTEREST

The following is a list of some other popular recreation sites in the Cascade Lakes Recreation Area and their corresponding locator letter on the map:

Northwest Forest Pass required

THE KEY TO
Having Fun

This key corresponds with the symbols in the corresponding editorial information.

- BIKING
- BOATING
- BOAT RAMP AVAILABLE
- CAMERA OPPORTUNITIES
- CAMPING
- FISHING
- GAS AVAILABLE
- GROCERIES
- HIKING
- HORSEBACK RIDING
- MOTOR BOATS ALLOWED
- PICNICKING
- RESORT
- RESTAURANT
- RV FACILITIES
- SAILING & WINDSURFING
- SWIMMING
- WATERSKIING

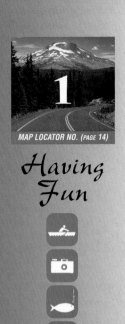

MAP LOCATOR NO. (PAGE 14)

Having Fun

The tranquil water of Mirror Pond makes it ideal for canoes and kayaks. Photo by Scott Schechtel

Drake Park

Downtown Bend is a step away from this scenic park!

A TRUE BEND LANDMARK, Drake Park is set in the heart of the city, bordering Mirror Pond, a tamed portion of the Deschutes River formed by a diversion dam at the northern edge of the park. Historically, it was the original site for two pioneer homesteads. Today, picnic tables and benches are scattered throughout the 12 acres of lush lawn and stately trees, and a playground for the kids is an easy walk across the footbridge to Harmon Park. Drake Park is the location for a number of events from live music to Saturday markets, from running races to canoe clinics. So convenient to downtown Bend, it is the ideal spot for relaxing after a morning of shopping and sightseeing in town.

ACTIVITIES:

BOATING: The tranquil water of Mirror Pond provides a pleasant place for boaters to practice their technique or simply float along and enjoy the scenery. Canoes, kayaks, skulls, and rubber rafts are the most popular water crafts used on the shallow pond.

CAMERA OPPORTUNITIES: Be sure to bring your camera as the park provides many opportunities for some great shots, whether it be the numerous ducks and geese always in evidence along the shoreline or in the water, the view of the Three Sisters in the distance, or a concert in session.

FISHING: Mirror Pond is a great place to let the kids try their luck. A special fishing event is held for kids each June.

PICNICKING: Numerous picnic tables are scattered throughout the park. Parking is available in the Mirror Pond Parking Lot (just west of the Franklin Avenue and Wall Street intersection) or along Riverside Boulevard.

AND FURTHERMORE: Although the park is home to a large number of "feathered," drakes, its namesake was Bend's founder, Alexander M. Drake. Unfortunately, the ever-present "droppings" of the ducks in the park have caused many headaches in recent years, thus the parks department discourages feeding the birds.

DIRECTIONS: *Located off Riverside Boulevard in downtown Bend, see Map Location #1 on the locator map on page 14.*

The reason for the name Mirror Pond is evident in this photo. Photo by David Morris

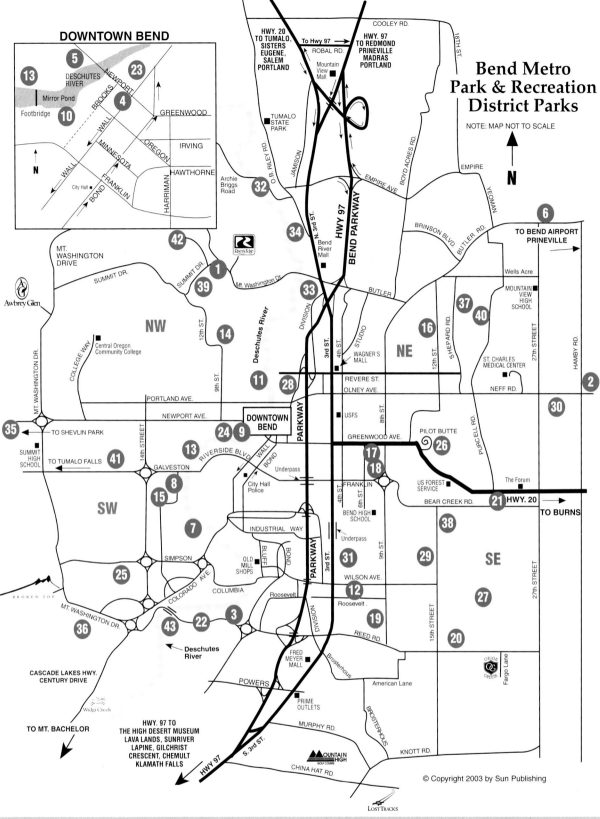

Bend Metro Park & Recreation District Parks

NOTE: MAP NOT TO SCALE

DOWNTOWN BEND

1. Awbrey Village Park	12. Vince Genna Stadium	22. Log Deck Park	33. Riverview Park
2. Big Sky Park and Sports Complex	13. Harmon Park	23. Pacific Park (Administration and Recreation offices)	34. Sawyer Park
3. Blakely Park Site	14. Hillside Park	24. Pageant Park	35. Shevlin Park
4. Brandis Square	15. Hixon Park Block	25. Park Services Center	36. Skyline Park Sports Complex
5. Brooks Park	16. Hollinshead Park	26. Pilot Butte State Park	37. Stover Park
6. Canal Park	17. Juniper Swim and Fitness Center	27. Pinewood Park	38. Sugarbowl Park
7. McKay Park	18. Juniper Park	28. Pioneer Park	39. Summit Park
8. Columbia Park	19. Kiwanis Park	29. Ponderosa Park	40. Sunburst Park
9. Dohema River Access	20. Larkspur Park Site and Bend Senior Center	30. Providence Park	41. Sunset View Park
10. Drake Park	21. Larkspur Trail	31. Railroad Park	42. Sylvan Park
11. First Street Rapids Park		32. River Run Trail	43. Woodriver Park I & II

© Copyright 2003 by Sun Publishing

2

MAP LOCATOR NO. (PAGE 14)

Having Fun

Lava Island, Dillon, and Benham falls

From this aerial shot, the wild whitewater of Dillon Falls on the Upper Deschutes River is very apparent. Photo by Geoff Hill

FOR A SPECTACULAR VIEW of untamed rapids, be sure to see any or all of these falls created when the normally placid water of the Deschutes River churns through the lava fields created during Central Oregon's fiery past. The name, Deschutes, means "River of the Falls,"

The changeable Deschutes River shoots down a narrow canyon, dropping almost 300 feet in a half-mile at Benham Falls. Photo by Don Burgderfer

and this section of the river accurately reflects the name.

At Lava Island, the first of the "falls" accessed from the Cascade Lakes Highway, the mighty Deschutes passes through a maze of jagged and broken lava, creating some exciting, rushing rapids. A trail from the parking area leads to a viewpoint along the river, but at some distance. However, the falls are difficult to view from the west side of the river as the main channel is on the east side and separated by a very large lava rock island. A small channel flows along the west side. Adventurous folks can wade the stream and scramble over rugged lava rocks to get a close-up view. (Good footwear is a must) In the fall, the turning aspen leaves makes this area especially spectacular.

Dillon Falls is a short distance from Lava Island. From the parking area, a scenic trail leads to a view of the quiet water turning into a churning rapid.

About 2.5 miles upstream is Benham Falls, the largest of the three rapids. This area can be accessed from several vantage points.

ACTIVITIES:

BIKING: One of the area's most notable mountain bike rides, the Deschutes River Trail follows the river from Lava Island to a turn-around point at Benham Falls. The very popular trail is heavily used in the summer and on weekends. Many of the forest service roads in the area are suitable for

18

RIGHT: This photo shows the beginning of the quarter-mile-long Lava Island Falls as viewed from the east side.
Photo by Doug Emerson

BELOW: The Deschutes puts on a different personality at Dillon Falls.
Photo by Don Burgderfer

mountain biking as well. Guide books and maps are available at the Forest Service office in Bend, local sports shops, and Sun Publishing.

BOATING: Untamed water and cataracts make most of this stretch of the Deschutes extremely dangerous for boaters. The safest section is the calm water between Benham and Dillon falls. Whitewater rafting trips, run by professional guides, are popular in the section of river between Dillon and Lava Island falls. These trips may be booked with experienced companies in Bend and Sunriver.

FISHING: Although much of the water is fast and dangerous along this stretch of river, there are some bank fishing opportunities for both fly and lure fishermen, no bait allowed in this section.

HIKING: Hiking trails follow the river and access numerous viewpoints. Several allow hikers to watch the whitewater rafters tackle the rapids. Trailheads are located at each of the falls.

HORSEBACK RIDING: Scenic guided trail rides along the river are offered at stables near The Inn of the Seventh Mountain.

PICNICKING: There are day use areas at each of the falls. A picnic area is located at the trail access point for Benham Falls when approached from the Lava Lands Visitor Center.

AND FURTHERMORE: Northwest Forest Pass is required at the trailheads in this area.

DIRECTIONS: *Located about 7 miles from Bend, see Map Location #2 on the locator map on page 14. Benham Falls can be reached from the Lava Lands Visitor Center (see page 53) as well.*

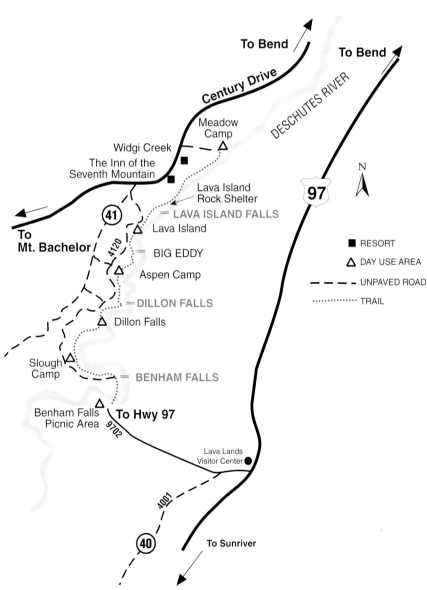

Having Fun

Swampy Lakes

THE NAME "SWAMPY LAKES" is evident when one takes advantage of the trails in this area. This trailhead/sno-park is located 15 miles from Bend just off the Cascade Lakes Highway. At an elevation of 5,500 feet, the area receives a lot of snow during the winter, often making early spring access a problem. This also accounts for the wet nature of trails especially in the spring and early summer. (Mosquitoes can be a problem!) From the parking area, there are a variety of well-marked trails from 2 to 10 miles in length and are open to mountain bikers and hikers. The area is an especially popular sno-park in the winter for cross country skiers. There are five shelters along the trails which are stocked with wood in the winter.

ACTIVITIES:

BIKING: The popular Swampy Lake Loop is an excellent introduction to single-track mountain biking. The loop is short, 2.5 miles, and has few obstacles. For those desiring a more challenging ride, there are numerous trails branching off of the main loop.

HIKING: Hikers share the same marked trails with the mountain bikers. Again, the trails offer a variety of levels of difficulty and length. Restrooms are available at the trailhead.

DIRECTIONS: *Located 15 miles from Bend, see Map Location #3 on the locator map on page 14.*

The mountain bike trails in the Swampy Lakes area offer challenges for bikers of all abilities.

The mountain bike trails at Swampy Lakes offer something for everyone from beginner to expert riders. Several loops begin and end at the trailhead, including the Swede Ridge Loop pictured above. Photo by Bob Woodward

Tumalo Mountain

The hike to the summit of Tumalo Mountain is well worth the effort!

AT 7,775 FEET, Tumalo Mountain may be dwarfed by Mt. Bachelor, but this mountain has a character of its own. When viewed from the east, the barren face that drops away from the summit can be seen for miles, especially in the winter when it is totally covered in snow. Just 20 miles from Bend, this mountain is a popular destination for hikers and cross country skiers. The panoramic view from the top includes views of Mt. Bachelor, the Three Sisters, Broken Top, Sparks Lake, the Tumalo Creek drainage, Bend, and even Smith Rock in the distance. The 1,200-foot elevation gain to the summit in 1.8 miles is well worth the effort! (Note: mountain bikers are prohibited from this trail.)

LEFT: Glimpses of Mt. Bachelor can be viewed from the trail.

BELOW: The mid-section of the trail passes through a colorful lupine-filled slope.

BELOW: The panoramic view of the Cascade mountains from the top of the mountain makes the trip worth the effort.

Photos by Geoff Hill

ACTIVITIES:

HIKING: This trail is considered "moderate to difficult" due to the elevation gain. The 4-mile roundtrip begins in the forest as a gradual but steady climb, then becomes more open the higher the ascent. The trail steepens rapidly for the final, steeply pitched last section. Hikers are advised to bring an extra shirt or windbreaker as it can be chilly and windy at the summit. Restrooms are located at the trailhead. Mosquitos can be a problem in the forested areas certain times of the year. A Northwest Forest Pass is required.

DIRECTIONS: *Located about 20 miles from Bend, see Map Location #4 on the locator map on page 14.*

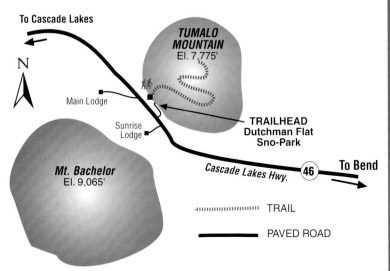

To Cascade Lakes

TUMALO MOUNTAIN El. 7,775'

N

Main Lodge

Sunrise Lodge

TRAILHEAD Dutchman Flat Sno-Park

Mt. Bachelor El. 9,065'

Cascade Lakes Hwy. 46 **To Bend**

·········· TRAIL

━━━━━━ PAVED ROAD

21

Having Fun

Mt. Bachelor

Central Oregon's favorite ski mountain is also a year-round resort.

WITHOUT A DOUBT, 9,065-foot Mt. Bachelor is Central Oregon's most familiar landmark. The mountain dominates the skyline, towering 3,000 feet above the surrounding forest plateau. It is one of the youngest of the Cascade mountains and may only be "resting" as "hot spots" have been detected during the winter indicating that the interior may still be warm. The mountain was originally named "Brother Jonathan" — the only brother to the Three Sisters — but the name was later changed to "The Bachelor" then "Bachelor Butte" and finally given mountain status as Mt. Bachelor.

With great snow often lasting well into June, the mountain is especially famous for incredible skiing. However it has also become a year-round playground with lodge services now available every season. A favorite summer activity is to ride a chairlift to panoramic views of Central Oregon. If you prefer to stay on the ground, a hiking trail to the summit starts at the Sunrise Lodge. Or bring a picnic basket, mountain bike, or volleyball and enjoy the recreational offerings at the base of the mountain.

Mt. Bachelor also plays host to a number of events throughout the year, ranging from professional and amateur ski races in the winter to concerts and mountain bike races in the spring and summer.

TOP: This is the most familiar view of Mt. Bachelor — snow-covered and ready for skiers. However, the resort at Mt. Bachelor welcomes visitors most of the year.

CENTER & RIGHT: Sightseers enjoy an outdoor barbecue on the deck at the Pine Marten Lodge.

Photos courtesy of Mt. Bachelor

Ride the lift up Mt. Bachelor for spectacular views of the surrounding mountain range and alpine lakes.

Summer sightseeing from Mt. Bachelor's Pine Marten lift generally runs from late June through Labor Day. The views are well worth the ride. The Forest Service offers free interpretive tours as well.
Photos courtesy of Mt. Bachelor

AMENITIES:

RESTAURANT & SPORTS STORE: During the summer season, one of the lodge restaurants opens and offers casual dining as well as twilight dinners and BBQs. Hours and menus vary so call in advance for information. One of the base lodges where visitors may purchase outdoor gear and souvenirs remains open as well.

ACTIVITIES:

BIKING: Mountain bikers enjoy the trails devoted to cross country skiing during the winter months as well as other trails and forest service roads accessible from this area. Bike rentals are available at the base lodge.

CAMERA OPPORTUNITIES: Sightseers who ride the lift up the mountain enjoy spectacular views of the surrounding mountain ranges and alpine lakes.

HIKING: Starting at Sunrise Lodge, a hiking trail leads to the top of the mountain. U.S. Forest Service interpretive tours are also scheduled for various times of the day; call ahead.

PICNICKING: Enjoy the scenery as well as lunch at one of the numerous tables near the base lodges.

DIRECTIONS: *Located 22 miles from Bend, see Map Location #5 on the locator map on page 14.*

Having Fun

Dutchman Flat

From Dutchman Flat, one can enjoy some impressive, close-up views of the Cascade mountains without even leaving the car! Photo by Geoff Hill

Crossing the wide open landscape called Dutchman Flat, visitors cannot help but be impressed by the panoramic mountain vistas opening before them.

BEYOND MT. BACHELOR the Cascade Lakes Highway crosses an unusual new landscape — a pumice desert. The Dutchman Flat area never accumulated much soil and is unable to provide the nutrients needed for the growth of many plants, thus resulting in a desert-like environment. Only the hardiest of plants survive here, such as pink pussypaws and yellow sulfur flowers.

Story has it that the prairie was named for a rancher of Dutch descent who grazed his livestock in the area. Caught by early snow, he was forced to winter here with his flock of sheep. Although the authenticity of this story is questioned, Dutchman Flat did gain notoriety as the site for the filming of many scenes in the movie titled "How The West Was Won" starring Kirk Douglas and Robert Mitchum.

Driving by Dutchman Flat, visitors are treated to some impressive close-up views of the Cascade mountains. Called a "badly shattered volcano" by geologists in the mid-1800s, Broken Top especially takes center stage.

There are no facilities at Dutchman Flat. During the winter, the road is closed here due to drifting snow from about mid-November until late May or June. However, cross country skiers and snowmobilers make good use of the snow-covered road and surrounding trails.

DIRECTIONS: *Located about 22 miles from Bend, see Map Location #6 on the locator map on page 14.*

Todd Lake

During the summer, beautiful wildflowers cover the meadow surrounding this small lake

ABOVE: Looking north in this aerial view, Broken Top (right), Middle and North Sisters loom above Todd Lake.

INSET: Stocked brook trout are the only game here.
Photos by Geoff Hill

RIGHT: A float tuber enjoys the solitude at Todd Lake.
Photo by Brian O'Keefe

THE FIRST OF A DOZEN LAKES along the Cascade Lakes Highway, Todd Lake lies below Broken Top Mountain in a gently sloping bowl rimmed with tall firs. At 6,150 feet, Todd is the highest of the lakes and covers approximately 45 acres with a maximum depth of 56 feet. The lake is a short walk from the parking area, located just a half-mile off the highway.

AMENITIES:

CAMPING: There is a small, secluded, no-fee campground with tent sites and outhouse, but no drinking water.

ACTIVITIES:

BOATING: With its calm tranquil water and spectacular views, Todd Lake is ideal for canoes, kayaks, and small pack-in boats. Motors are not allowed on this lake.

CAMERA OPPORTUNITIES: During the summer, yellow and purple wildflowers litter the meadow surrounding the lake. Excellent views of Mt. Bachelor and Broken Top dominate the horizon.

FISHING: Stocked brook trout are the only fish here. Float tubes and boats are useful, however anglers can fish or wade from the shoreline.

HIKING: Hiking trails lead off from the picnic and campground area and wind around the lake. Be sure to wear waterproof boots or shoes, especially in the early summer, as the many little streams and swampy areas along the trail make the going wet. Also be prepared for mosquitoes as they can be a problem certain times of the year. Hikers can access other trails into the Three Sisters Wilderness from the trailhead.

PICNICKING: A picnic area is located a short walk from the parking area.

HORSEBACK: Horse routes into the Three Sisters Wilderness may be accessed from the Todd Lake Trailhead.

DIRECTIONS: *Located 27 miles from Bend, see Map Location #7 on the locator map on page 14.*

Having Fun

Sparks Lake

LEFT:
Looking in one direction, Broken Top commands the skyline. From another (below), Mt. Bachelor dominates the view.
Photos by Geoff Hill

Bring your raft, canoe, kayak, or rowboat and explore the hidden coves and beaches of Sparks Lake.

A canoe is the perfect way to enjoy the scenery at Sparks Lake. South Sister rises in the background.
Photo by Don Burgderfer

THE REAL SPARKS LAKE is a hidden treasure few tourists ever find out about. At first glance, all you see is a broad, shallow, weedy body of water. However, if you continue to drive down the east side of the lake to the boat ramp, you'll be rewarded with a whole new perspective — a long channel of clear water lined by trees on one side and lava outcroppings on the other with South Sister towering in the background. The lake is slowly dying a natural death as it fills with sediment and transforms into a meadow, however, it is a hidden treasure worth exploring. Another reason to visit Sparks is to take the Ray Atkeson Memorial Trail, an interpretive trail commemorating Atkeson, Oregon's Photographer Laureate. *(See page 28.)*

AMENITIES:

CAMPING: There are two small campgrounds on the lake: Soda Creek Campground and Sparks Lake Campground. There are no fees and no drinking water at either site.

ACTIVITIES:

BIKING: Designated mountain bike trails are located at the Sparks Lake Trailhead, about .1 mile off the highway.

BOATING: Canoes, kayaks, and rafts are ideal on this large, shallow lake. Motors are allowed with a 10 mph speed limit, however low water levels late in the season may prevent their useage. A boat ramp is available at the end of the gravel road along the east side of the lake.

CAMERA OPPORTUNITIES: Numerous sites along the Ray Atkeson Memorial Trail provide opportunities for photographers. *(See following page.)*

FISHING: Sparks Lake is open to fly angling only. Cutthroat and brook trout are the main catch. A boat is helpful.

HIKING: Located about .1 mile off the highway, the Sparks Lake Trailhead has a large parking area and is the starting point for numerous popular trails in the area. The short, barrier-free Ray Atkeson Interpretive Trail *(See following page.)* is located further down the east side of the lake. Toilet facilities are available.

PICNICKING: Picnicking spots are available near the Atkeson trail area.

DIRECTIONS: *Located 30 miles from Bend, see Map Location #8 on the locator map on page 14.*

ABOVE: South Sister dominates the horizon at Sparks Lake, a shallow lake open for fly fishing only. Photo by Geoff Hill

BELOW: A fly angler tries his luck in one of the narrow channels winding through the Sparks Lake area. Photo by Brian O'Keefe

THE RAY ATKESON MEMORIAL TRAIL AT SPARKS LAKE

A photo wayside point and hiking trail honoring Ray Atkeson for his nationally acclaimed photography of the Oregon landscape have been created at Sparks Lake, an area he especially loved.

"It has a beauty all its own, standing out from any other place in the state of Oregon." These words of Ray Atkeson, Oregon's late Photographer Laureate, refer to the Sparks Lake area and are inscribed on a bronze plaque where Atkeson took some of his most famous photographs. The plaque is imbedded in lava rock just off the Ray Atkeson Memorial Trail at Sparks Lake. South Sister, Broken Top, and Devils Hill (a massive lava flow) form a dramatic background across the lake. It is here where Atkeson took his celebrated photographs of South Sister reflected in Sparks Lake.

Shortly before his death in the spring of 1990 at the age of 83, Atkeson, ill with cancer, was told that the people of Oregon wanted to create a memorial to him in honor of his nationally acclaimed photography of Oregon landscape and to his dedication to the preservation of natural beauty. Atkeson then requested that the memorial be in the vicinity of Sparks Lake, an area he especially loved for its outstanding beauty.

This view of Sparks Lake and South Sister was taken from a point along the Atkeson Memorial Trail. Photo by Don Burgderfer

The memorial, officially opened in the fall of 1994, consists of two main features: a photo wayside point and a hiking trail at Sparks Lake. The wayside, 1.2 miles along the Cascade Lakes National Scenic Byway past the entrance to Sparks Lake, offers picturesque views of the lake with Mt. Bachelor in the background. An interpretive exhibit here contains a biographical sketch of Atkeson and information on the geology, plants and wildlife of the area.

The hiking trail is an easy 2.5-mile loop that starts from the parking lot on the east side of the lake. It winds through a dense, evergreen forest, passes enchanting views of the lake and circles back to the trailhead. The trail is routed to focus on interesting geologic formations and viewpoints, with interpretive signs of the geological features. The first quarter of the trail is paved, making it wheelchair accessible to this point.

Deschutes National Forest representatives give guided geology tours along the Atkeson trail during the summer.

Ray Atkeson's photographic career spanned over 60 years and was largely responsible for placing Oregon "on the map." Sometimes called Oregon's unofficial ambassador, he was largely responsible for the growth of tourism in this state. Atkeson's photos were published in several volumes of large, hardbound, coffee table books. The large format allowed the reader to feel as though he were actually at the scene. Atkeson's photos have also appeared in *Life*, *National Geographic*, *National Wildlife*, and countless other publications.

It was Atkeson's hope that through publication of his work, people would enjoy the outdoors more and become aware of "this great American heritage that should be preserved as nearly as possible the way nature created it." The hiking trail and wayside is a fitting living memorial to Ray Atkeson, Oregon's legendary photographer.

Marge Kocher

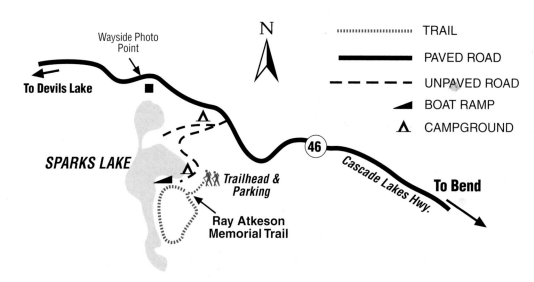

Devils Lake

THE DISTINCTIVE TURQUOISE TINT of the water caused by the sandy bottom of this shallow lake distinguishes it, the smallest of the Cascade lakes, from its neighbors. Easily seen from the highway, a large pull-out allows photographers a scenic viewpoint.

AMENITIES:

CAMPING: Devils Lake Campground offers walk-in tent sites for no charge. Outhouses are available but there is no drinking water.

ACTIVITIES:

BOATING: This small, shallow lake is ideal for canoes, kayaks, and small boats.

CAMERA OPPORTUNITIES: The extraordinary turquoise color of this crystal clear lake make it a favorite for photographers.

FISHING: Though this cold, clear lake does not grow fish rapidly, brook and stocked rainbow trout inhabit the lake. Still fishing from a boat and shore fishing are most effective.

HIKING: Many trails branch out from the Devils Lake Campground including one to the south shore of the lake. Others lead into the Three Sisters Wilderness where overnight camping permits are required. The trails lead to a number of glacial lakes and ponds accessible only by foot.

PICNICKING: A spot along the shore is a great place for a quiet picnic.

AND FURTHERMORE: A horse ramp, parking for stock trailers, and horse access to the wilderness trails are located adjacent to the campground.

DIRECTIONS: *Located 29 miles from Bend, see Map Location #9 on the locator map on page 14.*

LEFT: Easily viewed from the Cascade Lakes Highway, this cold, clear, turquoise blue lake is a popular wayside attraction. Devils Hill lava flow is in the foreground. Aerial photo by Geoff Hill

BELOW: This small, shallow lake is perfect for canoes, kayaks, and small boats. Photo by Bob Woodward

Having Fun

Crystal clear, turquoise blue water distinguishes Devils Lake.

Having Fun

Elk Lake

Beautiful mountain views and clear blue water greet visitors to Elk Lake. Photo by Geoff Hill

Elk Lake has become a mecca for windboards and sailboats.

BRING YOUR CAMERA when you visit Elk Lake! The colorful sails of the windboards and sailboats dotting the cold, clear, deep blue water of the lake against the prominent peak of South Sister in the background is a photographer's dream come true. The cool mountain breezes and wide, sandy shoreline make Elk Lake an ideal spot for water sports of all kinds. Elk has a surface area of 390 acres and a maximum depth of 75 feet. The lake is so transparent you can see the bottom clearly from any location on the surface.

AMENITIES:

CAMPING: There are three campgrounds are on the lake: Elk Lake Campground and Point Campground on the west shore, both with pressurized water systems, latrines, and use fees; and Little Fawn Campground on the southeast corner with a hand pump, latrines, and use fees. Little Fawn also has a group camp that can be reserved in advance.

GAS: Gas and metered propane may be purchased at the resort.

GROCERIES: Tackle, groceries, and cold drinks are available at the resort.

A USFS sign provides info about the lake; sailboats fill the moorage; and Mt. Bachelor rises in the distance.
Photo by Geoff Hill

RESORT: Elk Lake Resort, open year-round with the exception of a short period between seasons, offers fully furnished cabins with kitchens, fireplaces, and gas heat. A restaurant is located at the lodge for full meals as well as snacks. Boat rentals are also available (see below).

ACTIVITIES:

BIKING: Mountain bikers should pick up a Deschutes National Forest map to identify available trails and forest service roads accessible from this area.

BOATING: There are no obstacles to boating on Elk Lake. Boat launches are located at the resort and at Little Fawn and Point campgrounds. Canoes, paddleboats, and rowboats are available for rent at the resort as are fishing boats and motors. There is a 10 mph speed limit on the lake. The afternoon winds make sailing popular as well.

CAMERA OPPORTUNITIES: Spectacular views of Mt. Bachelor and South Sister, pine forested areas, and sandy beaches provide numerous opportunites for photographers at the lake.

FISHING: Elk Lake supports both stocked and naturally reproducing kokanee and brook trout. The most productive methods are still-fishing and trolling from boats.

HIKING: Trailheads are just on the other side of the Cascade Lakes Highway from the lake. The Pacific Crest Trail is one mile to the west of Elk Lake.

PICNICKING: Forest Service day-use facilities on the lake include Beach on the southwest corner, Little Fawn on the southeast corner, and Sunset View on the east shore.

SWIMMING: Sandy beaches for wading and swimming are located at Beach, Little Fawn, and Sunset View day-use areas.

WINDSURFING: Most windsurfing activity takes place at Sunset Cove, located on the east side of Elk Lake.

DIRECTIONS: *Located 33 miles from Bend, see Map Location #10 on the locator map on page 14.*

LEFT: Anglers fishing for brook trout have the most luck in water no deeper than 20 feet at Elk. Photo by Brian O'Keefe

BELOW: An aerial view of Elk Lake gives evidence to its wide open expanse and deep blue color. Photo by Geoff Hill

INSET: The afternoon winds at Elk Lake make it a popular destination for windsurfers. South Sister rises in the background. ©Jon Gnass/Gnass Photo Images

Having Fun

Hosmer Lake

WILDLIFE VIEWING OPPORTUNITIES abound at Hosmer Lake as the thick reeds and grass lining the lake and heather-covered islands provide excellent cover for fish and birds. A short drive off the highway, this long, narrow, shallow lake is one of the few western lakes stocked with Atlantic salmon.

AMENITIES:

CAMPING: There are two good campgrounds on the lake. Both have outhouses and charge fees; however, no drinking water is available.

ACTIVITIES:

BOATING: Typical craft seen at Hosmer include canoes, kayaks, float tubes, drift boats, and rubber rafts. Electric-only motor boats are allowed with a 10 mph speed limit. Boat ramps are avail-

ABOVE RIGHT: Aerial view looking east to west over this shallow lake and heather-covered islands. Photo by Geoff Hill
BELOW LEFT: Hosmer is a great place to take a canoe or kayak. Photo by Lana Young
BELOW RIGHT: Broken Top is visible from the heavily vegetated shoreline. Photo by Don Burgderfer

Large Atlantic salmon can be seen cruising in the crystal clear water.

able at both campgrounds: a concrete ramp at South Campground and a small slip at Mallard Marsh Campground.

CAMERA OPPORTUNITIES: Cascade views and abundant wildlife will not disappoint visitors.

FISHING: Hosmer is restricted to fly fishing only with a barbless hook, catch and release for the Atlantic salmon. Brook trout as well as Atlantic salmon live in the lake. As the shoreline is heavily vegetated, it is best to fish from a boat or float tube.

DIRECTIONS: *Located 39 miles from Bend, see Map Location #11 on the locator map on page 14.*

Little Lava Lake

Having Fun

The mighty Deschutes River begins its journey to the Columbia at Little Lava Lake

LITTLE LAVA LAKE IS MOST FAMOUS as the source of the mighty Deschutes River. Emerging from the lake as a tiny brook, the river begins its 252-mile journey to the Columbia River, dropping almost 4,800 feet along the way.

AMENITIES:

CAMPING: A small Forest Service campground on the lake has drinking water, outhouses, and a small boat ramp.

ACTIVITIES:

BIKING: Mountain bikers should pick up a Deschutes National Forest map to identify available trails and forest service roads accessible from this area.

BOATING: This is a good lake for small boats and rafts. Motors are allowed with a 10 mph speed limit. A small boat ramp is available.

CAMERA OPPORTUNITIES: Beautiful views of the Cascades dominate the skyline.

FISHING: Most people fish from a boat for stocked rainbow and native brook trout.

HIKING: A trailhead is located just south of the junction with the road to Lava Lake.

SWIMMING: A shallow wading area near the boat ramp is perfect for children.

DIRECTIONS: *Located 41 miles from Bend, see Map Location #12 on the locator map on page 14.*

ABOVE: Little Lava Lake is a great place to take a canoe or small boat. Photo by Bob Woodward

BELOW: Looking south in this aerial, the Deschutes River is seen emerging from Little Lava Lake. Photo by Geoff Hill

Having Fun

Lava Lake

"BIG" LAVA LAKE is one of several high Cascade lakes with excellent trout fishing as well as beautiful surroundings. The view from the lake is dominated by Mt. Bachelor, South Sister, and Broken Top. Created by flows of lava from Mt. Bachelor, Lava Lake covers approximately one-half square mile and is 30 feet deep at its maximum depth. At Lava Lake many visitors come to fish, although some come just to camp, enjoy the sights, or canoe this popular scenic area.

AMENITIES:

CAMPING: A Forest Service campground on the lake has drinking water, latrines, a fish cleaning station and a good boat ramp.

GAS: Gas and metered propane may be purchased at the resort.

GROCERIES: A full line of tackle, groceries, and ice cold drinks are available at the resort.

RESORT & RV FACILITIES: Lava Lake Resort offers an RV park with full hookup as well as showers and a laundromat.

ACTIVITIES:

BIKING: Mountain bikers should pick up a Deschutes National Forest map to identify available trails and forest service roads accessible from this area.

LEFT: The views from the shoreline at Lava Lake include many of the Cascade peaks. Looking north, Mt. Bachelor rises in the distance.

BELOW: Lava Lake Resort offers a variety of boats for rent and a good boat ramp.
Photos by Geoff Hill

The fish grow big in this rich, spring-fed lake, making it an excellent trout fishery. Photo by Geoff Hill

BOATING: Lava Lake is an excellent place for enjoying a day on the water. Canoes, paddleboats, and rowboats are available for rent at the resort as are fishing boats and motors. There is a 10 mph speed limit on the lake. Two boat ramps are available.

CAMERA OPPORTUNITIES: Be sure to bring your camera as the views from this lake are well worth preserving. Beautiful views of Mt. Bachelor, South Sister, and Broken Top dominate the far shorelines.

FISHING: Lava Lake has a well-deserved reputation as a "hot" trout fishing spot. The main catch are rainbow and brook trout. Peak fishing takes place early and late in the season. Still-fishing with bait, trolling, and fly fishing are the most popular methods. Floating devices are useful but not necessary.

HIKING: There are a number of easy trails starting at Lava Lake Resort. One leads to the headwaters of the Deschutes River where it flows slowly out of Little Lava Lake. A scenic trail starting on the east side of the lake near the boat launch winds above the shoreline through a forest of lodgepole pine and old ponderosa. You can follow this on to Hosmer Lake or retrace your steps back to the start. Other trails may be accessed from this area

PICNICKING: Enjoy the scenery as well as lunch at one of the day use tables near the lake.

DIRECTIONS: *Located 41 miles from Bend, see Map Location #12 on the locator map on page 14.*

The view from the lake is dominated by Broken Top, South Sister and Mount Bachelor.

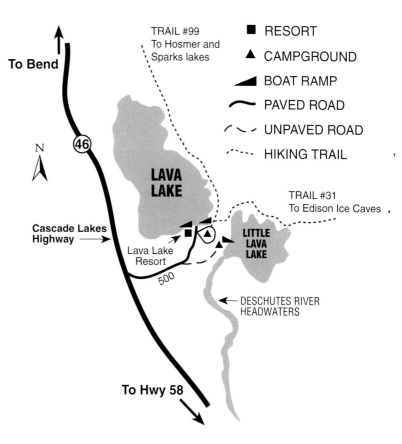

35

Deschutes to Wickiup

ALTHOUGH NAMED RIVIERE DES CHUTES (River of the Falls) by French-Canadian trappers, the Deschutes River begins its tumultuous journey to the Columbia River as a small, crystal-clear stream when it exits Little Lava Lake. Originally flowing westward, the river was forced by the growing Cascade mountains and flows of lava from the Newberry Volcano to change its course, detouring south before eventually flowing north to the Columbia. Along its 252 miles, the Deschutes changes moods and character as it twists and tumbles from an elevation of 4,739 feet above sea level to 186 feet when finally joining the Columbia. The uppermost seven miles from its origin at Little Lava Lake to Crane Prairie Reservoir is the only remaining free-flowing section of the river. It is narrow and swift and very picturesque, especially in July when a variety of wildflowers decorate the river banks and small islands. A short section of fast water flows from Crane Prairie to Wickiup Reservoir.

AMENITIES:

CAMPING: Deschutes Bridge Campground is located on this stretch of the river. Other Forest Service campgrounds are located on the river near Crane Prairie Reservoir, Cow Meadow above and Sheep Bridge below. All have vault toilets and river frontage. (See page 40 for Crane Prairie Reservoir). A day-use area with river access is located at Mile Camp.

ACTIVITIES:

FISHING: More like a creek than a river in this section, anglers would best be prepared with hip

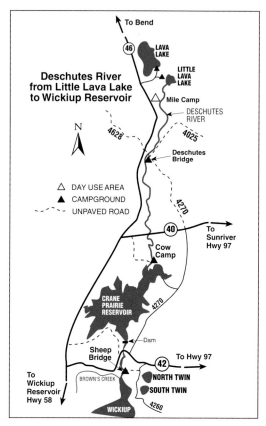

boots or waders, as early season water flows often spill over the banks and form marshy conditions. There are a number of spots along the highway that can be fished from the bank, however, these are high traffic areas and the fishing probably won't produce like it might off the beaten path. Certain restrictions and seasons are in effect for this area, so anglers are encouraged to check the Oregon State Fishing Regulations.

AND FURTHERMORE: Some spots along the river are marshy so water-proof boots and mosquito repellant come in handy!

DIRECTIONS: *This section of the Deschutes begins at Little Lava Lake, 41 miles from Bend and continues to Wickiup Reservoir. See Map Location #13 on the locator map on page 14.*

Little Cultus Lake

MORE SECLUDED than its neighboring "Big" Cultus Lake, much smaller Little Cultus Lake offers a quiet setting nestled in the pines on the opposite side of Cultus Mountain. Though over a rough road, the drive from Cultus Lake to Little Cultus is well worth the trouble. Unspoiled by many visitors, this lake is probably more in its natural state than any other of the high lakes.

Smaller and off the beaten track, Little Cultus Lake is ideal for a quiet, relaxing vacation.

AMENITIES:

CAMPING: Little Cultus Campground, located on the southeast corner of the lake, charges a fee and has RV and tent sites; a boat ramp; picnic area; and outhouses. There are more primitive, no-fee campsites on the northeast shore of the lake, accessible by the road into Deer Lake. All roads in the area are dirt or gravel.

ACTIVITIES:

BOATING: Motors are allowed on Little Cultus with a 10 mph speed limit. A boat ramp is available at the campground.

FISHING: There is good fishing for rainbow and brook trout at Little Cultus. The shorelines are gently sloping for easy wading or bank fishing. The deeper spots in the center of the lake must be accessed with floating devices.

HIKING: Hiking trails may be accessed from the Deer Lake Trailhead located adjacent to the campground. To hike to the top of Cultus Mountain follow Forest Service Road 640 which winds up Cultus Mountain.

PICNICKING: Enjoy the scenery as well as lunch at one of the picnic areas near the lake.

SWIMMING: The shallow area near the campground and boat ramp area is easily accessed for wading and swimming.

DIRECTIONS: *Located 54 miles from Bend, see Map Location #14 on the locator map on page 14.*

Nestled in the forest, Little Cultus Lake offers a peaceful setting for some good fishing, hiking, boating, and relaxing.
Photo by Geoff Hill

14

MAP LOCATOR NO. (PAGE 14)

Having Fun

Cultus Lake

IT'S HARD TO BELIEVE that the Chinook word "cultus" means bad or totally worthless when you gaze out at Cultus Lake, the largest natural Cascade lake. Stretching for three miles, the lake is surrounded by a dense pine and fir forest. The large expanse of open water makes Cultus especially popular for waterskiing, personal watercraft, sailing, and trout fishing; and swimmers appreciate the warm water and sandy beaches on the eastern and western shores. If water sports aren't to your liking, there are many excellent hiking and mountain bike trails, many that lead to smaller high lakes.

AMENITIES:

CAMPING: There are three Forest Service campgrounds located on the lake. Cultus Lake Campground offers RV and tent sites, drinking water, and a boat launch. Cultus North Shore and West Cultus Lake no-fee campgrounds at the north and far west end of the lake are accessible by boat, hiking, or horseback and have tent sites only and no drinking water.

GAS: Gas and oil may be purchased at the resort.

GROCERIES: A full line of tackle, groceries, and picnic supplies are available at the resort.

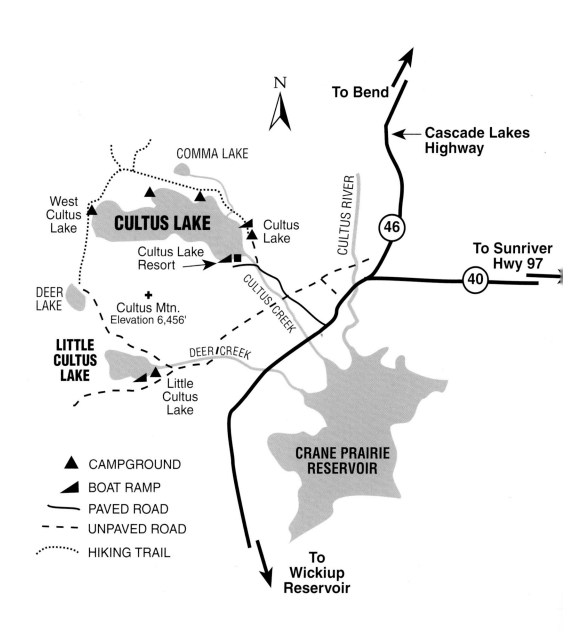

▲ CAMPGROUND

◢ BOAT RAMP

— PAVED ROAD

- - - UNPAVED ROAD

······· HIKING TRAIL

This large, open lake is especially popular for swimming and boating.

ABOVE: Cultus Lake is surrounded by pine and fir trees and bordered on the north and west by the Three Sisters Wilderness.

RIGHT: The lake is a popular recreation area with its long sandy beaches.

Photos by Geoff Hill

RESORT: Amenities available at Cultus Lake Resort include a lodge and restaurant, cabins, general store, boat rentals (see below), and boat ramp.

ACTIVITIES:

BIKING: Popular rides include a loop around the lake. Mountain bikers should pick up a Deschutes National Forest map to identify available trails and forest service roads accessible from this area.

BOATING: The wide open expanse and deep water allow a variety of boating activities at Cultus Lake. Canoes, rowboats, and kayaks are available for rent at the resort as are fishing boats and motors. Larger boats for waterskiing are here as well, as are personal watercraft.

CAMERA OPPORTUNITIES: The huge lake surrounded by pine and fir forest and sandy beaches offer numerous opportunities for photographers.

FISHING: Cultus Lake is noted for its large mackinaw (lake trout) living in the deep water. Rainbow and brook trout are also caught. Floating devices for trolling are most successful in this large lake.

HIKING: A three-mile trail into the West Cultus Campground starts at the Winopee Trailhead near the Cultus Lake Campground. Other trails branch off from this one for day hikes and backpacking in the Three Sisters Wilderness area.

PICNICKING: Picnickers can enjoy watching the activities on the water from day-use picnic sites near the resort and campground.

SAILING AND WINDSURFING: Sailing and windsurfing on the open water is best in the afternoon.

SWIMMING: Long sandy beaches with shallow water for swimming are located along the eastern and western shores.

WATERSKIING: The wide open expanse and deep water make Cultus Lake ideal for waterskiing all summer.

DIRECTIONS: *Located 48 miles from Bend, see Map Location #14 on the locator map on page 14.*

Having Fun

Crane Prairie Reservoir

BEFORE THE DESCHUTES RIVER was dammed in the 1920s to form a reservoir for irrigation purposes, Crane Prairie was a large meadow in which long legged cranes would fish. The trees surrounding the prairie were not logged before the meadow was flooded and now occupy 10% of the water's surface. Instead of being an eyesore, the abundance of dead wood has created a rich environment for fish and wildlife, especially numerous species of birds, including the potentially endangered osprey. To protect these birds, the reservoir has been designated as a special osprey management area. Visitors can view the birds from an observation point, located on the west side of the reservoir. Crane Prairie's namesake, the sandhill crane, continue to nest here as well.

AMENITIES:

CAMPING: A number of campgrounds are located at Crane Prairie including full hookups. Four Forest Service campgrounds are located on the lake. Crane Prairie Campground is the largest and offers RV, and tent sites, drinking water, and a good boat launch. Rock Creek, Quinn River, and Cow Camp (no drinking water) are smaller fee campgrounds with boat ramps.

GAS: Gas and oil may be purchased at the resort.

GROCERIES: A full line of tackle, groceries, and picnic supplies are available at the resort.

RESORT: Open from late April into October, Crane Prairie Resort is a full service RV park with showers, general store, boat rentals and boat ramp. Fishing guide services are available as well.

ACTIVITIES:

BIKING: Numerous forest service roads in the area are available for biking as well as a trail accessed at the Browns Mountain Bridge Day Use Area.

BOATING: Boat ramps are located at each of the campgrounds and the resort, the best being at the Rock Creek and Crane Prairie Campgrounds and the resort. A 10 mph speed

TOP: Fly fishermen try their luck on a calm day at Crane Prairie. Photo by Brian O'Keefe

BELOW: The facilities at Crane Prairie Resort include a marina, RV park, showers, and store with a full line of tackle and some grocery items. Photo by Geoff Hill

ABOVE: To enjoy this view of Crane Prairie Reservoir, one must hike to the top of Cultus Mountain.

LEFT: From the air, this view of Crane Prairie Resort shows a burn area north of the resort from a wildfire in the 90s. Photos by Geoff Hill

Fishing, camping, and birdwatching are the main reasons to visit Crane Prairie Reservoir.

Nesting osprey are a common sight at Crane Prairie.
Photo by Brian O'Keefe

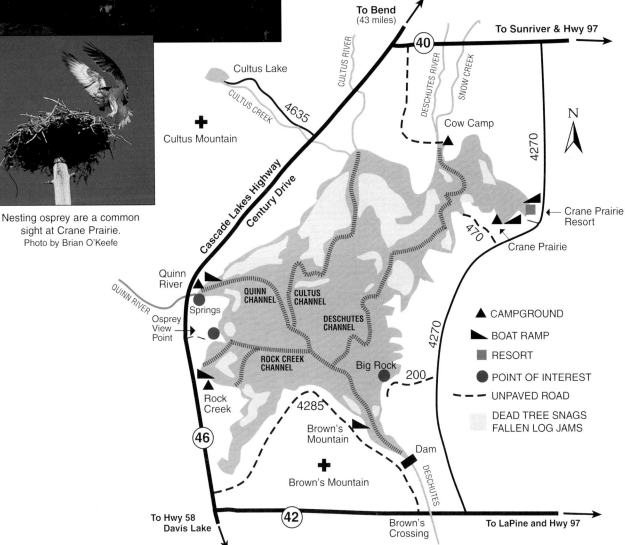

CRANE PRAIRIE RESERVOIR
Elevation 4,445'

To Bend (43 miles)

To Sunriver & Hwy 97

(40)

CULTUS RIVER

DESCHUTES RIVER

SNOW CREEK

Cow Camp

4270

N

Cultus Lake

CULTUS CREEK

4635

✚ Cultus Mountain

Cascade Lakes Highway

Century Drive

470

Crane Prairie Resort

Crane Prairie

Quinn River

QUINN RIVER

Springs

QUINN CHANNEL

CULTUS CHANNEL

DESCHUTES CHANNEL

Osprey View Point

ROCK CREEK CHANNEL

Big Rock

200

4270

▲ CAMPGROUND

◣ BOAT RAMP

◼ RESORT

● POINT OF INTEREST

- - - UNPAVED ROAD

▨ DEAD TREE SNAGS FALLEN LOG JAMS

Rock Creek

(46)

4285

Brown's Mountain

Dam

DESCHUTES

✚ Brown's Mountain

To Hwy 58 Davis Lake

(42)

Brown's Crossing

To LaPine and Hwy 97

41

FROM TOP:

A float tuber fishes open water while late afternoon sunlight glows off the snags. Photo by Brian O'Keefe

Despite the challenge from snags, publisher Geoff Hill caught a nice 20-inch rainbow, the most abundant species in the reservoir. Photo by Vicki Hill

From almost every direction, the Cascade mountains dominate the scenery. Photo by Geoff Hill

limit is enforced. Water levels fluctuate with the irrigation season, and weed beds and snags outside the main channels may create difficulties.

CAMERA OPPORTUNITIES: The wildlife and waterfowl as well as the Cascade views make Crane Prairie a photographer's delight. Common sightings include osprey, cormorants, terns, a variety of ducks, bald eagles, and sandhill cranes. The summer months are the best time to view the nests and feeding of the young osprey from the Osprey Observation Point. If you are lucky you may see the birds, known for their fish catching, as they plunge straight down with an impressive splash.

FISHING: The nutrient-rich water and insect life combined with the abundance of snags for cover make Crane Prairie a very productive fishery. Native and stocked rainbow trout are the main catch. The largemouth bass fishery is also popular. Brook trout, kokanee, whitefish, crappie, bluegill, and chub also inhabit the reservoir. Most anglers fish from boats as the shoreline is lined with snags and floating logs.

HIKING: A nature trail to the water is located at the Osprey Observation Point on the west bank of the reservoir. No trail fee is required to park. Another short trail begins at the Browns Mountain Bridge Day Use Area near the south end of the reservoir.

PICNICKING: Picnickers can enjoy watching the activities on the water from picnic sites near the resort and campgrounds.

SWIMMING: Swimming and wading in the shallow water is possible at the campgrounds, although the reservoir bottom is often quite muddy.

DIRECTIONS: *Located 45 miles from Bend, see Map Location #15 on the locator map on page 14.*

Twin Lakes

A boater enjoys the tranquil water at South Twin Lake. Motors are not allowed on either of the lakes. Sun Publishing file photo.

Calm water and good swimming beaches make both Twin Lakes a great place for families.

Sunbathers enjoy the large sandy beach and calm water at South Twin Lake. Photo by Geoff Hill

UNUSUALLY ROUND WITH NO DEFINED INLETS OR OUTLETS, North and South Twin Lakes are geological gems. Both lakes occupy volcanic craters which were created when rising hot magma met ground water, creating a boiling steam explosion which blasted a hole in the ground. The filled crater of North Twin is slightly larger than South Twin. Both are about 60 feet deep. South Twin Lake is the more "developed" of the two and gained notoriety when President Hoover stayed at the lake while on a fishing trip in 1940.

AMENITIES:

CAMPING: The two Forest Service campgrounds on South Twin have drinking water, latrines, boat ramps, and beach areas. North Twin Campground is more primitive with latrines, dirt boat launch, beach, but no drinking water.

GROCERIES: A full line of tackle, groceries, and ice cold drinks are available at the resort.

RESORT & RV FACILITIES: Twin Lakes Resort offers an RV park with full hookups, showers and laundromat (open to the public), a store, restaurant, rental cabins, and boat rentals (see below).

ACTIVITIES:

BIKING: Many mountain bike trails originate in this area. Bikers should pick up a Deschutes

Having Fun

National Forest map to identify available trails and forest service roads.

BOATING: No motors are allowed on either lake. Paddleboats, and rowboats are available for rent at the resort. Boat ramps are located at the resort and campgrounds.

FISHING: The main catch at both North and South Twin lakes are rainbow trout. Because the lakes are almost completely tree-lined, the winds are rarely a factor while fishing. Most anglers fish from boats and use bait. Angling from shore is also popular.

HIKING: Numerous trails may be accessed from the campgrounds at both lakes.

PICNICKING: Pick up supplies at Twin Lakes Resort and enjoy a picnic on the beach. A day-use area is available at South Twin Campground as well.

SWIMMING: Good swimming beaches are located at the resort and campgrounds.

DIRECTIONS: *North Twin Lake is 42 miles from Bend; South Twin is 44 miles. See Map Location #16 on the locator map on page 14.*

LEFT AND INSET: Twin Lakes Resort offers a store, cabins, restaurant, RV park, and boat rentals.

BELOW: Two Forest Service campgrounds with RV and tent sites are available at South Twin Lake. Campsites are more primitive on North Twin Lake.

Photos by Geoff Hill

Wickiup Reservoir

WHILE FISHING AND HUNTING in the area, Indians used the now flooded meadows at Wickiup Reservoir for camping. Their temporary huts were called "wickiups" and were made by putting up poles and covering them with brush, branches, or hides. Stockmen later adopted this name for the meadow. Some of the poles were still present when the Deschutes River was dammed in 1949 to form a reservoir and the name remained.

At 10,000 acres, Wickiup is the largest body of water along the Cascade Lakes Highway and is a popular recreation site for a variety of water-related activities.

AMENITIES:

CAMPING: There are six Forest Service campgrounds located on the shoreline at Wickiup: Sheep Bridge, Gull Point, North Davis Creek, Reservoir, Wickiup Butte, and Round Swamp. All have latrines and boat ramps; Gull Point and North Davis have drinking water. Three campgrounds are located on the Deschutes Arm of the reservoir: Sheep Bridge and South and West South Twin (see page 47).

RESORT & RV FACILITIES: The resort at South Twin Lake has easy access to the Deschutes Arm of Wickiup Reservoir (see page 47).

The rich warm water and cool deep channels produce BIG fish at Wickiup!

ABOVE: This photo of the Deschutes Arm of Wickiup was shot looking north, with South Twin Lake in the foreground and North Twin off to the right. Crane Prairie Reservoir and Cultus Mountain are in the background. Photo by Geoff Hill

RIGHT: This lucky angler caught a beautiful brown trout almost as big as she is. Wickiup is renowned for its large brown trout as well as good populations of kokanee and rainbow. Photo courtesy of John Garrison

Largest of the Cascade lakes, Wickiup Reservoir is noted for its variety of water sports and excellent fishing.

TOP: The character of the shoreline at Wickiup is as variable as the water level. Many stumps were left when the reservoir was filled … this one appears to be an octopus running along the beach.
Photo by Don Burgderfer

RIGHT: Wickiup is a great place to bring the kids and a boat!
Photo by Kim Hogue

ACTIVITIES:

BIKING: Numerous Forest Service roads are located around reservoir and accessing the campgrounds. Mountain bikers should pick up a Deschutes National Forest map to identify these and other trails available in this area.

BOATING: On the main body of the reservoir, there is no boat speed limit, and jet skis and waterskiing boats are popular. Boats are limited to 10 mph on the arms. Irrigation drawdowns during the summer often cause extreme water level fluctuations affecting the boating. Obstacles in the water emerge at low water, and caution is advised. Many of the boat ramps may not be useable in low water levels.

FISHING: The rich warm water and cool deep channels produce big fish at Wickiup, whose reputation for large brown trout is well known. Shore fishing is popular along the dam and shorelines of the arms; however, fishing from a floating device is most productive. Although boating may be diffi-

cult in some areas, the fluctuating water levels do not seem to affect the fishing; however, the prevalent afternoon winds will.

HIKING: There are numerous trails near the campgrounds and beach areas and along the shoreline.

PICNICKING: Enjoy the scenery as well as lunch at one of the numerous beaches.

WINDSURFING: Afternoon winds along the east end of the reservoir are almost a guarantee at Wickiup making it an excellent place for windsurfing.

SWIMMING: The shallow water and sandy beaches near the campgrounds are ideal for swimming and wading. Other sandy beaches are accessible around the reservoir.

WATERSKIING: The large open expanse makes waterskiing possible at Wickiup; however, boaters must be aware of the water fluctuations. The boat ramp at Gull Point is used mainly for speedboats.

DIRECTIONS: *Located 45 miles from Bend, see Map Location #17 on the locator map on page 14.*

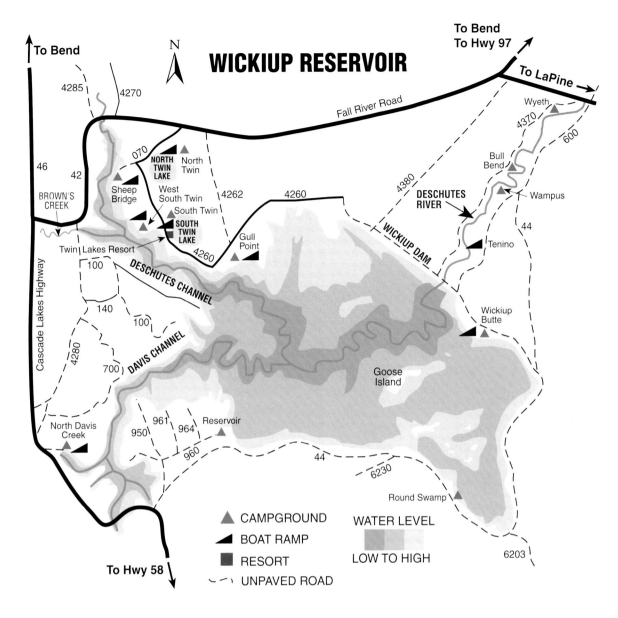

WICKIUP RESERVOIR

To Bend

To Bend
To Hwy 97

To LaPine

N

4285
4270

Fall River Road

46
42

4380

4370
600

Wyeth

Bull Bend

Wampus

DESCHUTES RIVER

44

Tenino

BROWN'S CREEK

070

NORTH TWIN LAKE

North Twin

Sheep Bridge

West South Twin

4262

4260

South Twin

SOUTH TWIN LAKE

Gull Point

Twin Lakes Resort

4260

WICKIUP DAM

Cascade Lakes Highway

100

DESCHUTES CHANNEL

140

100

Wickiup Butte

4280

700

DAVIS CHANNEL

Goose Island

North Davis Creek

961

964

Reservoir

950

960

44

6230

Round Swamp

6203

▲ CAMPGROUND

◢ BOAT RAMP

■ RESORT

UNPAVED ROAD

WATER LEVEL

LOW TO HIGH

To Hwy 58

Sunbathers enjoy a large sandy beach at Wickiup. Photo by Geoff Hill

Having Fun

Deschutes to Sunriver

THE DESCHUTES RIVER changes dramatically below Wickiup Dam tranquilly rambling left and right through miles of ponderosa forest and grass-lined banks dotted with wildflowers.

A scenic bend in the river below Wickiup Reservoir.
Photo by Geoff Hill

Highly accessible and easy to drift, this stretch of the river is popular for float trips. However, there are two areas that boaters must be aware of and avoid … Pringle Falls and Tetherow Log Jam. The flow varies with the irrigation season but runs mainly in one channel throughout this stretch. The area is easily accessed at a number of boat launches, campgrounds, and recreational areas.

AMENITIES:

CAMPING: Forest Service campgrounds along the river include: Bull Bend, Wyeth, Pringle Falls, and Big River as well as the LaPine State Recreation Area.

ACTIVITIES:

BIKING: Mountain bikers should pick up a Deschutes National Forest map to identify available trails and forest service roads accessible from this area.

BOATING: Drifting this section of river is a popular pastime, and a number of commercial guides are available for float trips in this area. One obstacle to be avoided is Pringle Falls, located between Wyeth Campground and the Tetherow Log Jam. A 5 mph speed limit is enforced for motor equipped boats.

CAMERA OPPORTUNITIES: Be sure to bring your camera as the wildlife abounds along the river.

FISHING: This part of the river is home to the best population of stream-inhabiting brown trout in the state. Other trout species and whitefish are available as well. Bank fishing and drift fishing are the most popular methods. Access is best above LaPine State Park where the river is bordered mainly by Forest Service land. Below the park and through Sunriver, homes line the banks, limiting angling from the bank.

PICNICKING: Picnickers can often find spots along the river near the various boat launches. Tables are available at the campgrounds and LaPine State Recreation Area. *(See page 51)*

DIRECTIONS: *See Map Location #18 on the locator map on page 14.*

Deschutes River from Wickiup Reservoir to Sunriver

N

△ DAY USE AREA
▲ CAMPGROUND
◣ BOAT ACCESS
◞◞ UNPAVED ROAD

To Mt. Bachelor
SPRING RIVER
To Bend
SUNRIVER
45
Harper Bridge
40
4220
97
To Crane Prairie Reservoir
General Patch Bridge
42
Fall River Hatchery
▲ Big River
42
FALL RIVER
LITTLE DESCHUTES
▲ Fall River
4360
LaPine State Recreation Area
Huntington Road
To Twin Lakes & Wickiup Reservoir
TETHEROW LOG JAM
PRINGLE FALLS
Pringle Falls
To East & Paulina Lakes & Newberry Crater
Wyeth
Bull Bend
44
4370
43
Wickiup Junction
Wickiup Dam
WICKIUP RESERVOIR
Tenino
To LaPine

Fall River

CRYSTAL-CLEAR AND SPRING-FED, Fall River flows east for eight miles emptying into the Deschutes River between Sunriver and LaPine. The river emerges from springs full-size with a steady flow and cold temperature. The banks are lined by meadows, pines, and willows and half is bordered by National Forest land. Fall River's pristine water supports a thriving hatchery for rainbow trout and is a popular fly fishing destination.

AMENITIES:

CAMPING: Fall River Campground is the only Forest Service campground on the river.

ACTIVITIES:

CAMERA OPPORTUNITIES: Be sure to bring your camera as the wildlife abounds along the river.

FISHING: Fall River is open to fly fishing only with trout species as the main catch. Many downed logs in the river provide cover for the fish. Access is easiest in the two miles above and below the fish hatchery. In 2002, an accidental fire retardant drop missed its target and spilled into the lower section of the river creating a massive fish kill that will take several years to recover.

HIKING: Several trailheads may be accessed from the highway for short hikes, including the fish hatchery and Fall River Falls.

PICNICKING: Spots for picnicking can be found along the river at the campgrounds as well as at the fish hatchery.

AND FURTHERMORE: A popular attraction just off the highway is the Fall River Fish Hatchery, operated by the Oregon Department of Fish and Wildlife. The hatchery produces some 140,000 legal size rainbow trout annually as well as other small fish for stocking Oregon's waters. Visitors are invited to view the fish production facilities and enjoy the scenic setting.

DIRECTIONS: *See Map Location #19 on the locator map on page 14.*

Having Fun

ABOVE: The river shows a variety of personalities, from calm, quiet water to riffles, rapids, and a waterfall. Photo by Geoff Hill

RIGHT: Fall River holds some beauties! Photo by Brian O'Keefe

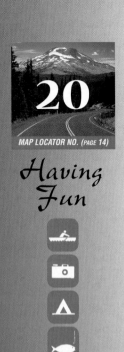

Having Fun

Little Deschutes River

This winding, twisting river is a tributary to the "big" Deschutes.

THE LITTLE DESCHUTES RIVER slowly meanders 120 river miles to cover just 30 land miles from its origin north of Miller Lake in the Mount Thielsen Wilderness to its convergence with the big Deschutes River, just south of Sunriver. Marshy areas line much of the river, and water levels are greatly influenced by irrigation withdrawals. About 90% of the river is bordered by private land so access is limited. The Cascade Lakes Highway crosses the Little Deschutes shortly after Big River Campground on the big Deschutes River.

AMENITIES:

CAMPING: The only Forest Service campground is Rosland Campground, situated about 2 miles north of LaPine.

ACTIVITIES:

BOATING: The slow current is great for floating in a raft, innertube, canoe, or kayak. Access, however is limited. The upper river above the town of Crescent offers some access off of Highway 58.

CAMERA OPPORTUNITIES: Photographers enjoy numerous bird and wildlife sightings.

FISHING: Anglers fish for trout in this easily waded river, though again, access is limited. Floating and fishing is the easiest way.

DIRECTIONS: *See Map Location #20 on the locator map on page 14.*

ABOVE: The Little Deschutes meanders and winds through Central Oregon.
Photo by Jim Horyza

LEFT: The river has a lot of undercut banks and a soft bottom. Fishing from the bank is limited by large willow bushes and other vegetation.

Photo by Geoff Hill

LaPine State Recreation Area

ABOVE AND RIGHT: Numerous camping facilities are available at LaPine State Park including rental cabins and yurts, a community hall, and shower house. Photos by Geoff Hill

LEFT: Since this photo was taken, a log fence was built to surround and separate "Big Tree" from all intruders who would touch and walk around its trunk. Photo courtesy of Oregon Department of Transportation

HOME TO "BIG TREE," Oregon's largest ponderosa pine, the LaPine State Recreation Area is well worth a visit. Standing over 161 feet tall and 28.9 feet around, this magnificent pine dwarfs all surrounding trees and is thought to be over 500 years old. Located on the banks of the Deschutes River, the tree is not the only reason for a stop at this state park. Picnicking, boating, camping, and fishing are among the activities enjoyed in this large subalpine pine forested area.

AMENITIES:

CAMPING: LaPine State Park camping facilities are open year-round offering 95 full-hookup campsites, a dump station, five cabins, and three yurts. Reservations may be made in advance.

ACTIVITIES:

BOATING: LaPine State Recreation Area is the take-out point for a popular eight-mile floating section of the Deschutes beginning below Pringle Falls (with one short portage around the Tetherow Log Jam). From the park rafters and canoeists can continue drifting downstream for 16 miles to Sunriver, enjoying the wildlife and scenery along otherwise inaccessible stretches.

CAMERA OPPORTUNITIES: Aside from the "Big Tree," photographers enjoy numerous bird and wildlife sightings in the park.

FISHING: A number of good fishing spots along the Deschutes are easily accessed throughout the park. Brown and rainbow trout are the main catch.

PICNICKING: Enjoy a picnic by the river at the day-use area.

DIRECTIONS: *See Map Location #21 on the locator map on page 14.*

Having Fun

Lava Cast Forest

THE LAVA CAST FOREST is an incredible tribute to the power of the volcano. About 6,000 years ago, hot, molten lava from the Newberry Volcano overwhelmed a forest of pine trees, burning away the wood but cooling quickly enough to form a coating around each tree. The charred trees remained upright and eventually rotted away, leaving a hollow mold or cast. The Lava Cast Forest covers about five square miles and is one of the largest collections of lava tree molds in the world.

Now a part of the Newberry National Volcanic Monument, the Lava Cast Forest geological area was established by the Forest Service in 1942 to protect the lava trees and tree molds in the area. Open year-round, weather permitting, visitors can study these unique formations firsthand while wandering a one-mile, paved loop trail.

ACTIVITIES:

CAMERA OPPORTUNITIES: The unique lava cast formations and landscape provide numerous photo opportunities.

HIKING: A one-mile, paved, barrier-free, self-guided interpretive trail gives visitors access and information about this area. A vault toilet is located at the trailhead. A Forest Service Trail Pass is required for parking.

DIRECTIONS: *Located about 24 miles south of Bend, the forest is nine miles off of Highway 97 on Forest Road 9720, an unpaved road east at the junction to Sunriver. See Map Location #22 on the locator map on page 14.*

The name Lava Cast Forest is not quite accurate since what we see are hollow molds of absent trees.

RIGHT: A visitor examines one of the many specimens in the Lava Cast Forest. Photo by Doug Emerson

BELOW: Lava knocked down this tree before destroying it. The white paper is about one-foot square. Photo by Robert A. Jensen

Lava Lands Visitor Center

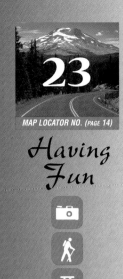

An aerial view of Lava Butte from the south. The visitor center is in the foreground between the highway and the lava flow. Photo by Robert A. Jensen

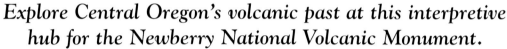

Explore Central Oregon's volcanic past at this interpretive hub for the Newberry National Volcanic Monument.

BEGIN TO UNDERSTAND the geologic and botanic wonders of Central Oregon's lavaflows and cinder cones at the Lava Lands Visitor Center located adjacent to the 500-foot Lava Butte. About 7,000 years ago, the butte was created after an eruption from cinders and lava bombs settling back into the vent. The prevailing winds caused a larger buildup on the northeast side. Lava broke through the base of the cone and covered over nine square miles, consuming the forest and impacting the Deschutes River.

Automated displays, exhibits, and slide shows in the visitor center vividly describe the geology that formed the volcanic buttes and recent lava flows. Behind the center are two self-guided interpretive trails: over the lavaflow, and through a pine plantation. A small gift shop offers books and related materials on the area.

Visitors may drive to the summit of Lava Butte for a breathtaking view of the Cascade Range and the acres of lava surrounding the butte. A small visitor center at the summit will further explain the geology of the area and pinpoint some of the landmarks seen from this viewpoint. An interpretive trail circles the crater rim. Due to limited parking at the summit, cars are allowed during controlled time slots.

Operated by the Forest Service, the Lava Lands Visitor Center is a part of the Newberry National Volcanic Monument. The visitor center is open from mid-April until mid-October. Spring and fall days of operation and hours vary, so visitors are advised to call for specific information. During the summer, the center is open daily.

AMENITIES:

VISITOR CENTER: A small gift shop, restrooms, drinking fountains, and snack machines are located at the center. A Forest Service Trail Pass is required for parking.

ACTIVITIES:

CAMERA OPPORTUNITIES: The unusual geologic formations and spectacular views from the summit of Lava Butte make this area a favorite for photographers.

HIKING: There are three short self-guided interpretive trails, two accessed from the visitor center and one from the top of the butte.

PICNICKING: Enjoy the scenery as well as lunch at one of the numerous tables adjacent to the visitor center. Be wary of the numerous hungry ground squirrels! Please don't feed them!

DIRECTIONS: *Located about 11 miles south of Bend on Highway 97, see Map Location #23 on the locator map on page 14.*

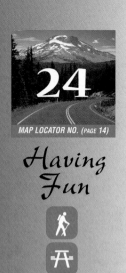

Having Fun

Lava River Caves

A UNIQUE ATTRACTION left by the volcanoes of Central Oregon's past are the lava tubes or caves. These caves were formed when the exterior crust of the flowing molten lava would cool and solidify while the interior lava remained hot and continued to flow, draining away to leave a hollow tube. The Lava River Cave is one example of these ancient lava tunnels. Over one mile long, the cave extends in two directions from the entrance. Located adjacent to Highway 97, the road is built right over it.

Brochures are available for a short self-guided walk through the main tunnel. Be prepared to see some spectacular formations formed by remelted lava dripping from the ceilings and walls. The cave remains a chilly 42°F year-round, so visitors are advised to dress warmly.

The Lava River Cave is a part of the Newberry National Volcanic Monument, operated by the Forest Service. The cave is open from mid-May until mid-October. Spring and fall days of operation and hours vary, so visitors are advised to call for specific information. During the summer, the center is open daily. A Forest Service Trail Pass is required for parking.

ACTIVITIES:

HIKING: There is an easy 1.2-mile roundtrip trail through the main tunnel. Hikers are advised to dress warmly as the cave temperature is a constant 42°F. Lanterns are available for rent.

PICNICKING: Tables and vault toilets are located adjacent to the parking area.

DIRECTIONS: *Located about 12 miles south of Bend off Highway 97, see Map Location #24 on the locator map on page 14.*

These caves are unique reminders of Central Oregon's fiery past.

Lava River Cave is the longest known uncollapsed lava tube in Oregon.
Photo courtesy of the Oregon Department of Transportation.

The High Desert Museum

The High Desert Museum describes itself as "more of an expedition than exhibition."

BELOW (clockwise from top): A young visitor draws water from the well at the homesteaders' cabin.

Visitors can observe animals in their natural setting. River otters are among the favorites.

The exhibits begin along the path to the entrance to the museum.

Photos courtesy of The High Desert Museum

NO VISITOR TO CENTRAL OREGON should leave without seeing The High Desert Museum. This is not a museum of stuffed creatures … it is a living museum designed to promote a better understanding of the arid Intermountain West. Located on 40 acres, the museum offers both indoor and outdoor participation-oriented exhibits and living displays about the local, cultural, and natural history of the area.

The 50,000-square foot indoor museum includes the Earl A. Chiles Center on the Spirit of the West, which features an exhibit named the Hall of Exploration and Settlement. Here visitors take a walk through time beginning at dawn with the Native Americans and ending at dusk with the cowboys. Detailed dioramas incorporating the sense of sight, sound, and smell depict various periods of history. These include a hard rock ore mine; high desert ranch complete with bunkhouse and blacksmith shop; and a complete western community with general store, harness shop, and bank.

Another favorite indoor highlight is the 2,500-foot desertarium where a variety of live high

The High Desert Museum is not a museum of stuffed creatures; it is a living museum designed to promote a better understanding of the high desert region.

desert wildlife such as burrowing owls, kangaroo rats, and collared lizards make their home.

Art lovers will enjoy several galleries in the museum featuring historical, Indian, and contemporary art from the area, one of which is constantly changing with traveling exhibits.

Heading outdoors, visitors can observe animals in their natural setting along a half-mile trail. River otters, porcupines, and birds-of-prey are among the wildlife easily viewed from the paved path. Other exhibits along the trail include a reconstructed settler's cabin, a forestry exhibit, turn-of-the-century sawmill, and covered wagons. These are just a few of the exhibits, many of which are staffed with trained volunteers to answer your questions.

Throughout the year, the museum holds special demonstrations, celebrations, and festivals as well as classes, workshops, and field excursions that combine adventure with fun.

Located six miles south of Bend off of Highway 97, the non-profit museum is open every day except Thanksgiving, Christmas, and New Year's Day. An admission fee is charged. Call ahead for prices, interpretive program schedules, and special events: 541-382-4754.

AMENITIES:

MUSEUM FACILITIES: A café, gift shop, restrooms, and education center are located in the main entry lobby. Picnic tables are available adjacent to the parking area.

DIRECTIONS: *Located 6 miles south of Bend on Highway 97, see Map Location #25 on the locator map on page 14.*

TOP: An authentic stagecoach is on display in the Hall of Exploration and Settlement, designed to give museum visitors a better understanding of the history of the Intermountain West.

CENTER: A volunteer demonstrates the spinning wheel during one of the museum's special days.

BOTTOM: (left) The exhibits include many Indian artifacts such as these baskets. (right) The museum is home to several owl species.

Photos courtesy of The High Desert Museum

Surrounded by beautiful campsites in thick forests, Odell Lake is one of the blue giants of the high Cascade lakes.
Photo by Geoff Hill

The BLUE GIANTS
of the Willamette Pass

A Trip to Four Big Lakes: Crescent, Odell, Waldo, and Davis
With a Side Trip to Salt Creek Falls

The following is a one-day trip to four big lakes: Crescent, Odell, Waldo, and Davis with a side trip to Salt Creek Falls. Three of these lakes are not on the Cascade Lakes Highway, and none are covered individually in this book; however they are well worth a visit when one is touring in Central Oregon.

By Don Burgderfer
(Updated and reprinted from Cascades East magazine)

TUCKED AWAY IN THE SOUTHWEST CORNER of the Deschutes National Forest, just east of the Cascade summit, along State Highway 58, lie the three largest natural lakes within the forest. Odell, Crescent, and Davis lakes, and just west of the summit, Waldo Lake, the blue giants of the Willamette Pass, together form our destination for this tour. Pack a picnic lunch, leave early, and plan to spend a full day enjoying this scenic tour.

Heading south on U.S. Highway 97 from Bend, we quickly enter the ponderosa pine forests of the area, climb past Lava Butte and the lava flows a few miles out, and continue southwest past turn-offs to other well-known spots such as the Lava River Caves, Sunriver, Fall River, East and Paulina Lakes, and Pringle Falls.

In the LaPine area we cross open meadows, while the timber type has changed to mainly lodgepole pine. Approximately 46 miles from our start we come to Gilchrist, formerly a company-owned town of the Gilchrist Timber Company. A mile farther is the town of Crescent.

To reach our four destination lakes, you can continue on south along U.S. 97 another ten miles to the junction of Highways 97 and 58, then back northwest on 58, or turn west at Crescent onto paved forest road 61 which will cut about 12 miles off your trip, each direction. Assuming we all want to save fuel, we'll turn at Crescent.

This forest road passes through a dozen miles of ponderosa pine, crosses Crescent Creek, a tributary of the Little Deschutes River, and joins Highway 58 about 14 miles from the U.S. 97/State 58 junction.

At Highway 58, turn northwest; drive only slightly over three miles and you'll enter the community of Crescent Lake. Here you'll find restaurants, groceries, service stations, fishing tackle, and information.

TO GET TO CRESCENT LAKE ITSELF, turn west and follow the signs two miles.

Less than a mile farther is the northern tip of the

lake and Crescent Lake Lodge. This lodge has cabins, a restaurant, store with tackle and groceries, and rental boats. In addition they can arrange for horses and provide information on hiking, fishing, or other local activities.

Crescent Lake is circled by forest roads, allowing access to all parts of the shoreline. Going clockwise, there are campgrounds on the east shore at Simax Beach; along the south shore at Contorta Point and Spring Creek; on the west shore at Tranquil Cove and Tandy Bay; and back at the north point, along the west side of the outlet stream, with a campground appropriately called Crescent Lake. There are boat launching areas at Spring Creek and Crescent Lake campgrounds.

This lake is at an elevation of 4,839 feet. The surface area is 3,600 acres, and the deepest spot is 280 feet. The fisherman will be interested in the kokanee and the rainbow, brown, and lake trout found here.

The best-known fish at Crescent Lake is the lake trout or mackinaw. Fish to over 30 pounds have been taken there, with many in the the 20-pound class. The area is also an excellent starting point for hikes to high country lakes to the south and west, or into the Diamond Peak Wilderness area to the north. The famed Oregon Skyline Trail, part of the Pacific Crest Trail system, touches the west end of the lake, allowing the hiker good access to nearly unlimited miles of hiking or horseback riding through superb scenery.

The second lake on our tour of the Willamette Pass blue giants is Odell.

From Crescent Lake, return to Highway 58 and turn west. Barely two miles up this highway you hit the southeast end of Odell Lake. From there you are about 70 miles from Eugene.

Odell, at 4,788 feet elevation is only slightly lower than Crescent. At 3,600 acres, it is the same size; and at 282 feet in depth, it is just two feet deeper.

Highway 58 parallels the northeast shore of Odell Lake for its full five-mile length. The shore opposite is followed by the Southern Pacific railway line.

There are two lodges at Odell Lake, one at each end. At either you can obtain accommodations, supplies, fishing tackle, rental boats, and motors.

This lake has a reputation for getting extremely rough when the winds come up, so anyone venturing onto the lake in a small boat should be well advised to

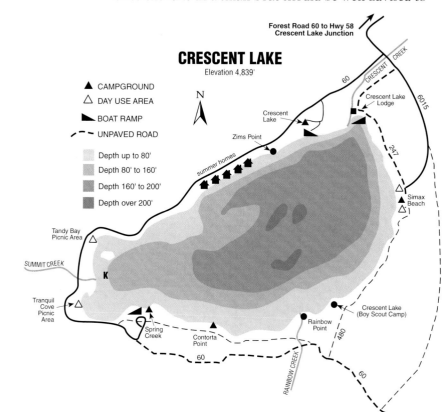

CRESCENT LAKE
Elevation 4,839'

▲ CAMPGROUND
△ DAY USE AREA
◣ BOAT RAMP
--- UNPAVED ROAD

Depth up to 80'
Depth 80' to 160'
Depth 160' to 200'
Depth over 200'

Forest Road 60 to Hwy 58
Crescent Lake Junction

CRESCENT CREEK

Crescent Lake Lodge

Crescent Lake

Zims Point

summer homes

Simax Beach

Tandy Bay Picnic Area

SUMMIT CREEK

K

Tranquil Cove Picnic Area

Spring Creek

Contorta Point

Crescent Lake (Boy Scout Camp)

Rainbow Point

RAINBOW CREEK

LEFT: The brilliant blue-green water of a "low" Crescent Lake is evident in this aerial shot, photographed looking east. Photo by Geoff Hill

ABOVE: The mackinaws grow big at Crescent. Photo by Rick Arnold

head for shore quickly when the winds increase. The lake also has a reputation for excellent fishing for kokanee, rainbows, lake trout, and the endangered and protected bull trout; and the lake trout of Odell Lake match the lunkers of Crescent for size. As with Crescent, this Odell has given up many mackinaws over 30 pounds, with many taken over 20 pounds each year. The state record catch is held here at Odell.

The Skyline Trail skirts the west end of the lake, making this another excellent starting point for hikes into the Diamond Peak Wilderness area or to hike-in lakes to the north.

Five campgrounds rim the lake. Odell Creek campground is near the Odell Lake Lodge at the southeast end. Traveling around the lake in a counterclockwise direction, we find Sunset Cove and Princess Creek campgrounds, along Highway 58. At the northwest end, within a mile of the summit of the Willamette Pass, a paved road follows the lake's shoreline around the west end and part way down the southwest shore. This roads leads to Shelter Cove Resort, Trapper Creek and Pebble Bay campgrounds.

LET'S CONTINUE ON TO WALDO LAKE. Leaving Odell turn west on Highway 58, you'll leave the Deschutes National Forest and head over the summit a short three miles to road 5897, the 13-mile paved road heads north to Waldo Lake.

You may opt to take the two-mile side trip to Salt Creek Falls before heading into Waldo. It is well worth the few minutes it will take.

You have to know a little about Waldo Lake to appreciate how really unique it is. At first sight, you are impressed at how big it is. And you are right! Waldo is the second largest natural lake in Oregon (only the Klamath Lake/Agency Lake complex is larger). The lake is six miles long, covers ten square miles and has almost 22 miles of shoreline. It holds about 800,000 acre-feet of water and is on the edge of a 37,162-acre wilderness area managed by the Willamette National Forest. The lake is at an elevation of 5,414 feet, the highest of the four lakes we'll visit, and is just west of the Pacific Crest National Scenic Trail.

This aerial view of Odell Lake looking south shows Shelter Cove Resort and Diamond Peak. Photo by Geoff Hill

Before releasing this trophy bull trout, an endangered species, this angler posed for the camera. Photo by Steve Kroll

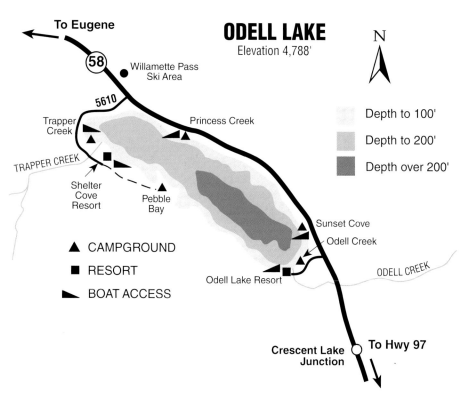

This high elevation gives some clue as to why the main recreational period at the lake is fairly short — usually from about July 1 to October 1, before and after which the snow may prevent visitation.

Geologist say that the Waldo Lake basin was scooped out by glaciers about ten- to twelve-thousand years ago. Those glaciers must have scratched the earth pretty hard because, at 420 feet deep, Waldo is the second deepest lake in Oregon (only Crater Lake, at 1,932 feet, is deeper). The lakes' great depth and the exceptional clarity of its water result in a beautiful cobalt blue color and the ability to frequently see the bottom at depths of 100 feet or more. The remarkable clarity of the lake is attributed to its chemically pure water and the resulting lack of any great amount of plankton. Scientists claim that Waldo is one of the purest lakes in the world with a water quality likened to that of fresh rainwater. The biological activity within the lake is so low that Waldo is said to be ultraoligatrophic, or "little nourished." Because of its elevation, great depth and short summers, Waldo's surface temperature usually ranges from 59°F to 64°F in the summertime.

For those who enjoy splashing in cold water, the eastern shore has by far the most sandy beaches; many portions of the western shore are rocky and may be quite steep. Waldo is surrounded by thick stands of douglas fir, hemlock and pine trees, and huckleberry bushes. A 20-mile loop trail encircles the lake for hiking and mountain biking. While the beaches are delightful, at any given time, some of them may be infested with mosquitoes. We have found that simply by moving to a different beach we are sometimes able to escape the pesky critters. Why they would be so thick at one beach and hardly in evidence at another one a few hundred yards away is a mystery.

The U. S. Forest Service spent several million dollars building camping and boating facilities for visitors at Waldo. There are three campgrounds on the eastern shore, while the rest of the lake is accessible only by boat or trail. The southernmost campground is Shadow Bay, with 103 sites. More toward the northeast part of Waldo are Island Campground (60 sites) and North Waldo Campground (63 sites). They are all modern campgrounds and have piped water, flush toilets, and boat ramps. Occupancy is limited to ten days. The rest of the lakeshore area is maintained in a primitive undeveloped state.

Areas at this elevation can be subject to sudden weather changes, so visitors should come prepared with warm and waterproof clothing. And, for goodness sakes, don't forget your mosquito repellent! Then you will be ready to enjoy one of the most up-to-date and least crowded campground areas in Oregon, not to mention one of the purest lakes in the world!

Now let's return to Highway 58 and back past Odell and Crescent Lakes to Road 61 again. Follow 61 about four miles until it junctions with Road 46, turn left and follow the signs about six miles to the fourth lake in our cluster of "Blue Giants" … Davis Lake.

This lake is completely different in character from the others. It is at nearly the same elevation as Crescent and Odell, 4,400 feet, and is only slightly smaller at 3,200 acres. But there the similarity ends. The depth is only 25 feet, less than 1/10 the depth of either Crescent or Odell. There are no resorts on Davis Lake.

Davis Lake is roughly circular in shape, with the deepest water beginning at the northeast side just off

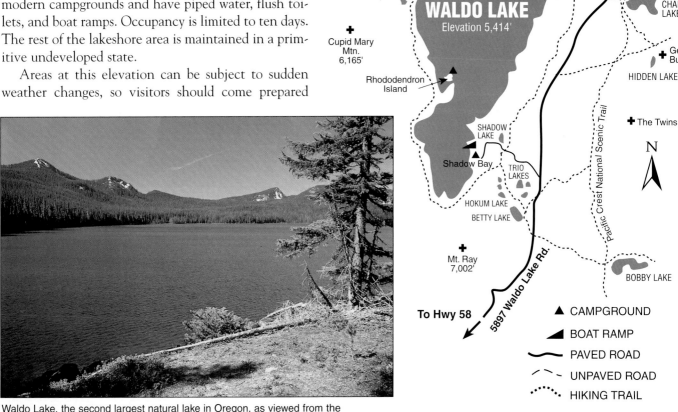

Waldo Lake, the second largest natural lake in Oregon, as viewed from the eastside shore. Photo by Don Burgderfer

Open for fly fishing only year-round, Davis Lake holds some big rainbows. Photo by Brian O'Keefe

the lava flows. Odell Creek enters the lake from the south. These are the two best places to fish — off the lavas or in the creek channel. Davis Lake is justly famed for the large rainbow trout found there. The rainbows will average 17 or 18 inches, with many of them going to four pounds and over.

This is a flyfishing-only lake and is closed to angling from a motor-propelled craft. Anyone fishing Davis Lake, or any waters of the state for that matter, should get a copy of the current Oregon Sport Fishing Regulations. These are available from most sporting goods stores and other places that sell hunting and fishing licenses.

There are three campgrounds on Davis Lake. Each side of the mouth of Odell Creek has one, appropriately named West Davis Lake and East Davis Lake. The Lava Flow Campground is along the east shore at the south edge of the lava flow. There is a boat ramp at the Lava Flow Campground.

You can return to Bend from Davis Lake by various routes. The easiest is to follow Highway 46 north about five miles where it joins Century Drive. Follow the signs back to U.S. 97. Or follow Century Drive on north past Elk Lake, right into Bend. The distance by either route is about the same.

Anyone traveling in the Deschutes National Forest should pick up a forest map from any U.S. Forest Service office. The supervisor's office is in Bend on Highway 20 directly south of Pilot Butte, or stop at the Bend/Fort Rock Ranger District Office at Red Oaks Square on Third Street in Bend. A forest map will show you routes, road numbers, locations of campgrounds and boat launch sites, and other facilities.

A once-over-lightly tour of these four lakes can be made in a day's time, but once you have sampled the fishing and beauty of these places, you'll want to return again, more frequently, and for longer periods. Fortunately they are close and readily accessible, these four blue giants of the Willamette Pass.

Salt Creek Falls

Travelers over the Willamette Pass, Highway 58, or anyone visiting in the area of Crescent, Odell, or Waldo lakes, should pause a few moments to view one of our state's more beautiful waterfalls.

Photo by Geoff Hill

Salt Creek Falls is in a deep, verdant canyon right alongside Highway 58. The falls is 286 feet in height, plunges over a rocky rim of dark-gray basalt and drops into a steep canyon covered with heavy, lush vegetation. The scene from the turn-off viewpoint is through an opening in the tall timber of the area.

Salt Creek itself begins only a few miles above the falls, the result of many small tributaries which drain the west slopes of the Cascade summit. Some of these tributaries come from Upper and Lower Marilyn and Gold lakes, a mile or two north of the highway. Salt Creek then flows on northwestward to join the Middle Fork of the Willamette River near Oakridge.

The maps also show a tiny lake, less than a quarter-mile from the falls, on the side away from the highway, with the intriguing name of Too Much Bear Lake. One wonders where this name came from. Did some early berry picker find the area crowded with bruins?

Salt Creek Falls is 61 miles southeast of Eugene. Those visiting the falls from the vicinity of Odell Lake have a much shorter trip.

From the northwest end of Odell Lake, it is just seven miles to the falls. Along the way you pass the Willamette Pass Ski Area on your right, and cross over the summit itself. Within two miles you begin to cross several of the small tributary streams that eventually flow together to make up Salt Creek. By the time all these waters reach the site of the falls, a pretty fair stream is produced, terminating in the beauty of the falls itself.

The Deschutes Arm of Wickiup Reservoir flows by South Twin Lake. Photo by Geoff Hill

Jewels of the Central Cascades

A Visit to Four Cascade Lakes: Crane Prairie Reservoir, North and South Twin Lakes, and Wickiup Reservoir

The following is a one-day driving tour of four lakes at the south end of the Cascade Lakes Highway. As this tour is intended to be done in one full day, the information in the following article is an overview of the highlights along the highway. For further details on the amenities and activities of a specific area, refer to the related articles on individual areas on the preceding pages.

By George W. Linn
(Updated and reprinted from Cascades East *magazine)*

THE CASCADE LAKES ARE LIKE A BEAUTIFUL PIECE OF INDIAN-MADE TURQUOISE. By itself, each lake is like a blue-green gemstone as it reflects the smog-free sky. Then, just as the Indian silversmith enhances the inner beauty of the turquoise, Nature has created its own settings to enhance the deep color of the lake. Stately pine trees with roots imbedded in the lake's shoreline reach toward the sky. Thousands, if not millions, of birds bring a touch of life. And, most of all, the magnificent mountains of the Cascade range tower in the background, reflecting their silvery images in the turquoise blue of the shimmering lakes. These lakes are the jewels of the Cascades.

Four of these lakes form a cluster at the south end of the Cascade Lakes Highway. These four have a special character all their own; because, generally, they are the first to free themselves of winter's snow and ice. Early season fishermen flock to them, anxious to wet a line after a long winter's lay-off. These four are Crane Prairie Reservoir, North and South Twin lakes, and Wickiup Reservoir.

We begin the tour to the "Jewels of the Central Cascades" at the junction of U.S. 97S and U.S. 20E in Bend. Heading south on U.S. 97, our climb is imperceptible but definite. In the first 11 miles to the base of Lava Butte, we have climbed 900 feet. If you have an extra half hour or so, take time to tour the Lava Lands Visitor Center at the base of Lava Butte. *(See page 53.)* It's well worth it.

We continue on U.S. 97 south to Wickiup Junction which is the southern terminal point of the Cascade Lakes Highway. At Wickiup Junction, the Highway (designated Forest Service Route No. 43 here) heads west into the heavily wooded Deschutes National Forest after passing by several recreational land developments and crossing the Little Deschutes River which twists and turns its meandering way through a relatively flat meadow.

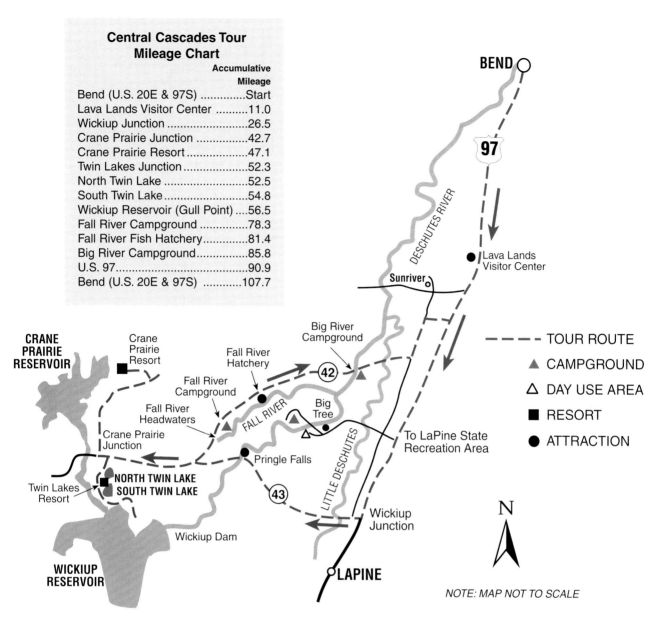

Central Cascades Tour Mileage Chart	
	Accumulative Mileage
Bend (U.S. 20E & 97S)	Start
Lava Lands Visitor Center	11.0
Wickiup Junction	26.5
Crane Prairie Junction	42.7
Crane Prairie Resort	47.1
Twin Lakes Junction	52.3
North Twin Lake	52.5
South Twin Lake	54.8
Wickiup Reservoir (Gull Point)	56.5
Fall River Campground	78.3
Fall River Fish Hatchery	81.4
Big River Campground	85.8
U.S. 97	90.9
Bend (U.S. 20E & 97S)	107.7

BEND

97

DESCHUTES RIVER

Lava Lands Visitor Center

Sunriver

Big River Campground

Fall River Hatchery

Fall River Campground

CRANE PRAIRIE RESERVOIR

Crane Prairie Resort

Fall River Headwaters

FALL RIVER

Big Tree

Crane Prairie Junction

Pringle Falls

To LaPine State Recreation Area

LITTLE DESCHUTES

- - - - - TOUR ROUTE
▲ CAMPGROUND
△ DAY USE AREA
■ RESORT
● ATTRACTION

Twin Lakes Resort

NORTH TWIN LAKE SOUTH TWIN LAKE

43

Wickiup Junction

Wickiup Dam

WICKIUP RESERVOIR

N

LAPINE

NOTE: MAP NOT TO SCALE

A few miles later, we cross the Deschutes River at Pringle Falls where a series of rapids send the river into a frenzy of whitewater as it dances and leaps over boulders. To the left, Pringle Butte stands like a sentinel, 700 feet over the surrounding terrain. Follow the Highway as it turns into Forest Service Road 42.

The turn-off to Crane Prairie Reservoir onto F.S. 4270 is well marked. Our destination is Crane Prairie Resort, which sits at the tip of an inlet at the extreme northeastern portion of the lake.

Crane Prairie Resort is the typical lakeside facility providing boats, a boat dock, boat launching area, bait, tackle, and basic groceries for the campers in the resort's RV park or the adjacent Crane Prairie Campground. Incoming boats meet outgoing boats, headed for the main body of the lake and their favorite fishing spots.

"Where did you catch those beauties? What are they biting on?" There is a continual exchange of information in the boat dock area.

Peering up over the horizon to the north, the South

Ringed by pine forests, the only open area at North Twin is the beach and boat ramp on the north shore. Photo by Geoff Hill

Sister, Broken Top, and Mt. Bachelor form the backdrop, a constant invitation to the photographer, as are fleecy clouds which gather over the lofty peaks.

Birds are everywhere. Of course, everyone expects to see osprey, because Crane Prairie is an Osprey Management Area. There is nothing quite like watching an osprey circling over the water, then making a plunging dive low into the water as it grasps a good-sized trout in its talons. It then zooms upward carrying the fish that weighs almost as much as it does, and there is always an element of suspense as the osprey changes its grip on the trout in mid-flight before heading back to its nest. If an eagle happens by during this drama, an aerial battle ensues, with the osprey usually losing his fish to the larger eagle.

It's easy to spend an hour or even a full day watching the myriad species of birds at various points along the lake, but we have three more lakes to visit on our tour; so we double back on Route 4270 and 42 to the turn-off to Twin Lakes and Wickiup Reservoir.

Whereas both Crane Prairie and Wickiup are man-made lakes formed by damming the Deschutes River, the Twin Lakes are natural lakes formed by explosive volcanic eruption caused when molten rock encounters ground water, throwing out lava fragments and hot mud in a circular pattern. They are known as *maar* (a German word) lakes or *tuff ring* lakes. Surprisingly, both Twin Lakes and Fort Rock some 50 miles to the southeast were formed by the same type of volcanic action.

As one might surmise by its formation, North Twin Lake is almost a perfect circle, less than half a mile in diameter. With the exception of a Forest Service campground at the north edge of the lake and a cleared boat launching area nearby, the North Twin is virtually unspoiled by man.

As one might suspect, the South Twin is truly a twin of the North Twin. *(Is that statement really necessary?)* The South Twin is almost the identical size and shape of the North Twin, but it is more developed by man. It, too, has a campground; and it also has a boat

The Cascade Lakes are like a beautiful piece of turquoise jewelry.

Each lake is like a blue-green gemstone around which Nature has created its own setting to enhance the deep color of the lake.

ABOVE:
Cultus Mountain is one of many viewed from Crane Prairie Reservoir.
Photo by Geoff Hill

FAR LEFT:
Kids love the sandy beaches surrounding Wickiup Reservoir.
Photo by Kim Hogue

LEFT:
Crane Prairie Reservoir is a favorite destination for anglers.
Photo by Brian O'Keefe

Fall River is a favorite with fly fishermen. Photo by Brian O'Keefe

dock and a cozy lodge on its south shore. In spite of their size, both Twin Lakes are well known for fishing. Powered boats are not allowed on either lake.

Just a stone's throw from the South Twin is the northern shore of Wickiup Reservoir. They are so close, in fact, that one's first impression is that they are the same lake; but they are not connected in any way.

Wickiup is a large — some five or six miles long and when full four miles wide — in years when the water level is high, that is. In as much as Wickiup provides irrigation water for much of Central Oregon's farmlands, the water level fluctuates greatly from season to season and year to year.

Because of its size, Wickiup accommodates large numbers of fishermen each year. When the lake is full, it is a beautiful lake with large expanses of open water making it an ideal spot for water sports.

The Forest Service maintains at least five campgrounds on the shore of Wickiup Reservoir and four boat launching areas. While it does not have the view of the Cascades enjoyed from lakes farther to the north, Wickiup is large enough to provide its own beauty. In a good year for water levels, it is the largest of all the Cascade lakes.

Rather than retrace our tour from Bend via Wickiup Junction, let's take a different route back.

From Wickiup Reservoir, head back past the Twin Lakes and turn east (right) on F.S. 42. Continue on this road (often called Fall River Road) past the junc-

tion with the Pringle Falls road (your incoming route F.S. 43). This keeps you on the west side of the Deschutes River for quite a few miles through beautiful forests.

This route parallels the Fall River for about five miles, from the Fall River Guard Station to the Fall River Fish Hatchery, which is operated by the State of Oregon. From that point, Fall River swings east (as you continue northeast) and joins the Deschutes two miles after Fall River Falls. The Fall River Campground is located near the Fall River Guard Station.

One of the interesting aspects of the drive through this area is the number of cinder cones visible. These relics of the era when Central Oregon was virtually a volcanic inferno dot the landscape, as do numerous examples of lava flows.

The foot bridge across the Deschutes River at Big River Campground is especially photogenic, with the rushing Deschutes River underneath it. After crossing the Deschutes, you are in privately owned land for the most part. You pass several interesting recreational developments, as well as at least two large ranches. Just before the highway swings east toward U.S. 97, you pass within a quarter mile or so of Sunriver.

When you reach Bend and have a chance to reflect on the day's tour, it may very well occur to you that you have spent a half or a full day in clean, clear, smog-free air … something that city dwellers have almost forgotten.

The Crater That Isn't A Crater
NEWBERRY CRATER
A One-Day Driving Tour of the Newberry Crater Area

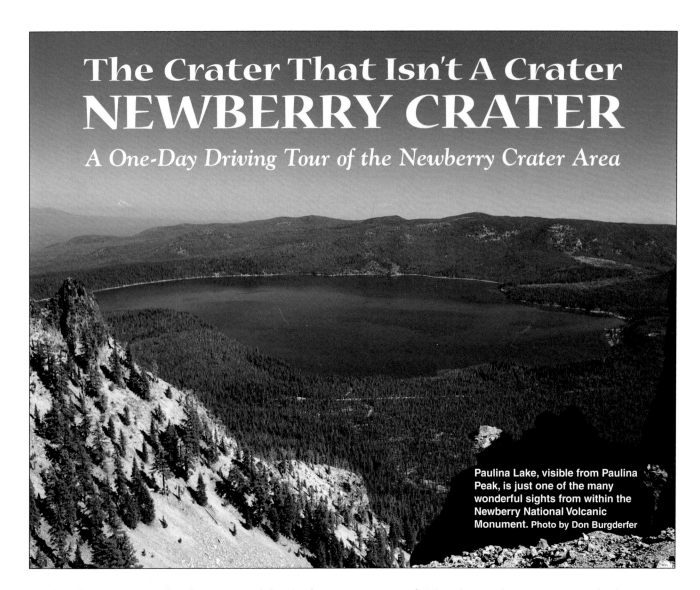

Paulina Lake, visible from Paulina Peak, is just one of the many wonderful sights from within the Newberry National Volcanic Monument. Photo by Don Burgderfer

The following is a one-day driving tour of the Newberry Crater area with stops at many of the attractions along the way. As this tour is intended to be done in one full day, the information in the following article is an overview of the highlights.

By George W. Linn
(Updated and reprinted from Cascades East *magazine)*

THE ICE AGE, IN OREGON, BEGAN SOME one-million years ago. Snow fields at higher altitudes became thicker and thicker until they finally grew into massive, permanent glaciers. Coincidental with the beginning of the Ice Age, increased volcanic activity in the low-lying Cascades began from Mt. Rainier in Washington to Mt. Shasta in California. As layer after layer of lava cooled and solidified, the volcanic peaks grew higher and higher. Thus, we see the birth of today's Oregon Cascade Range — Mt. Hood, Mt. Jefferson, Three Fingered Jack, Mt. Washington, the Three Sisters, Broken Top, Mt. Bachelor, Diamond Peak, Mt. Thielsen, Mt. Scott, and Mt. McCloughlin.

Just south of Bend, another giant, volcanic peak towered over the horizon. From its base which measured 25 miles in diameter, it reached up some 9,000 to 12,000 feet above sea level — approximately the same height as the ice-covered giants of the Cascades. Even though this peak no longer exists today, we call it Mt. Newberry.

In many ways Mt. Newberry was formed in the same way as the volcanoes of the Cascades. Molten lava was forced up from the bowels of the earth until it surfaced and hardened, but the core of the peak remained in molten state. However, Mt. Newberry had one flaw — or series of flaws. Many faults and fissures were underneath the mountain's base, and these vents "siphoned off" the molten lava from its core. Lava Butte and its 6,000-acre lava fields came from the heart of Mt. Newberry, as did Pilot Butte and some 200 other volcanic cones for many miles in all directions from the giant mountain. Many of the spectacular lava flows of Central Oregon, including the one that created the unique Lava Cast Forest, originated in Mt. Newberry. Consequently, Mt. Newberry became a hollow shell, drained of its molten supporting material.

Just as the Ice Age was drawing to a close some 10,000 years ago, only "yesterday" in geological time,

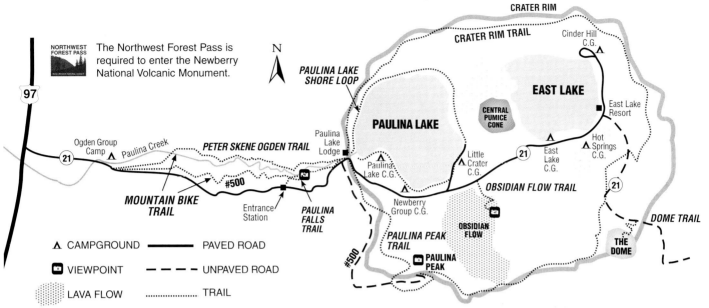

The Northwest Forest Pass is required to enter the Newberry National Volcanic Monument.

N

CRATER RIM

CRATER RIM TRAIL

Cinder Hill C.G.

PAULINA LAKE SHORE LOOP

EAST LAKE

CENTRAL PUMICE CONE

PAULINA LAKE

East Lake Resort

Paulina Lake Lodge

Little Crater C.G.

East Lake C.G.

Hot Springs C.G.

Ogden Group Camp   Paulina Creek   PETER SKENE OGDEN TRAIL

97

21

Paulina Lake C.G.

OBSIDIAN FLOW TRAIL

21

MOUNTAIN BIKE TRAIL

#500

Entrance Station

PAULINA FALLS TRAIL

Newberry Group C.G.

OBSIDIAN FLOW

DOME TRAIL

#500

PAULINA PEAK TRAIL

PAULINA PEAK

THE DOME

△ CAMPGROUND   ▬▬▬ PAVED ROAD

◻ VIEWPOINT   - - - UNPAVED ROAD

⬡ LAVA FLOW   ·········· TRAIL

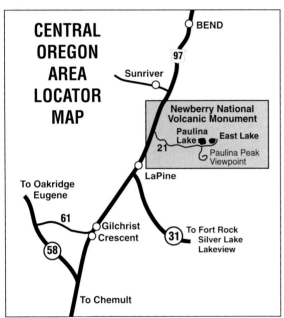

CENTRAL OREGON AREA LOCATOR MAP

BEND

97

Sunriver

Newberry National Volcanic Monument

Paulina Lake   East Lake

21   Paulina Peak Viewpoint

LaPine

To Oakridge Eugene

61

Gilchrist Crescent

58

31   To Fort Rock Silver Lake Lakeview

To Chemult

Newberry Crater Tour Mileage Chart

Accumulative Mileage

Bend (U.S. 20E & 97S)	Start
Lava Lands Visitor Center	11.3
Paulina Lake Turnoff	23.8
Paulina Creek Falls	36.7
Paulina Peak Summit	40.9
Paulina Lake Lodge	`45.6
Obsidian Flow	49.4
East Lake Campground	51.4
East Lake Lodge	53.2
Cinder Hill Campground	54.7
U.S. 97	74.0
Bend (U.S. 20E & 97S)	97.2

TOP: The twin falls of Paulina Creek Falls are worth the stop during your visit. Photo by Scott L. Staats

RIGHT: In 1993, Guy Carl set a state record for a "rod and reel" caught brown trout at Paulina Lake: 36 inches long; 27 pounds, 12 ounces. However, in 2002, a 28-pound, 5-ounce brown set a new record. Photo by Ross Martin

ABOVE: A young boy examines obsidian at Big Osidian Lava Flow. A signed path leads visitors through the flow.
© Jon Gnass/Gnass Photo Images

RIGHT: Views of Paulina Peak are visible from many points along the shoreline of East Lake. Photo by Geoff Hill

the awakened shell collapsed with an earthshaking roar that must have been absolutely awe-inspiring. Pre-historic Indians living in caves near Fort Rock, almost 30 miles to the south, were driven from their homes in terror. The top 3,000 to 6,000 feet of Mt. Newberry simply disappeared, leaving a depression some four to five miles wide.

This gigantic collapse brought on renewed volcanic activity which lasted for some 8,000 years. Dozens of volcanic cones were built up within the depression. Lava streamed from fissures opened up on the sides of the once mighty peak. One large cone in almost the exact center of the depression divided it into two distinct parts. Melting snows and underground springs of hot sulfur water created two of Oregon's most beautiful lakes on each side of the center cone.

Sometime during this 8,000-year period of volcanic activity, three distinct obsidian flows spread through the depression. One of these is considered to be one of the world's largest obsidian flows. The spilling obsidian from a vent high on the rim formed frozen cataracts of black, volcanic glass which attract geology students form all over the world.

Today, we call what is left of the once mighty mountain "Newberry Crater." However, in geological terms, it is *not* a crater — instead, it is a *caldera*.

The two bodies of water within the caldera are known as Paulina Lake and East Lake. The highest portion of the original mountain's shell is called Paulina Peak. Towering 8,000 feet above sea level, it is a reminder of the mighty mountain which was once

the highest peak in Oregon east of the Cascade Range. When Newberry Crater was discovered by Peter Skene Ogden in 1826, there were no fish in either lake; but careful stocking has turned Paulina and East lakes into two of Central Oregon's favorite fishing places. The area has become one of Central Oregon's most popular recreational centers for fishing, boating, camping, hiking, sightseeing, and snowmobiling. This is our primary destination on the tour to "The Crater That Isn't A Crater."

THE TOUR BEGINS IN BEND AT THE INTERSECTION of U.S. 97S and U.S. 20E. Continue south on U.S. 97 to the Lava Lands Visitor Center. We recommend a stop at the Visitor Center for two reasons. First, the imposing cone of Lava Butte and all of the surrounding fields of lava came from the heart of Mt. Newberry and helped lead to its collapse. Second, the displays in the Visitor Center will give you a better understanding of the extensive volcanic activity which Central Oregon has experienced. *(See page 53.)*

After our orientation visit at Lava Lands Visitor Center, continue south on U.S. 97 for approximately 12.5 miles to the well-marked Paulina Lake turn-off onto Forest Service Road No. 21 which is paved all the way up the base of Mt. Newberry.

It's only 13 miles to Paulina Lake through what used to be some of the most beautiful forest land in Oregon, before the pine beetle damage and wildfires struck the area. The climb is gradual but steady. From Paulina Prairie (at the turnoff from U.S. 97) to

Paulina Peak, the remnant rim of Mount Newberry, rises above Paulina Lake.
Photo by Geoff Hill

Paulina Lake, you climb over 2,100 feet.

Just as you reach the "top," you will see the Paulina Creek Falls picnic area. Don't pass up this stop. In the first place, if you brought a thermos of coffee, you won't find a more delightful place to relax for a few minutes than the tree-shaded picnic grounds. But, not more than a couple of hundred feet from the paved road, two forks of Paulina Creek take suicidal leaps over a cliff of lava to form side-by-side twin waterfalls. A sturdy fence separates the picnic area from the precipitous cliff.

The vantage point at the top of Paulina Creek Falls also gives you a magnificent view of the Cascade Range and the Deschutes River country far below. From this viewpoint, you are only 1,500 feet below the elevation of Mt. Washington, so you have a panoramic view which can be matched by few easily accessible points in Central Oregon. On a clear day, you can see some of the lakes along the Cascade Lakes Highway.

After leaving Paulina Creek Falls, continue on until you come to the turnoff for Paulina Peak Summit. From the falls, it is only a little over four miles to the top. But it is four miles of the most spectacular driving you will find anywhere in the state.

A word of caution, however. It is a precipitous drive. The views are awe-inspiring. The trip up is via a paved road, narrow at times, and no guard rail. Before starting the trip to the top, it must be fully understood that the driver is not a sightseer. The best solution is for one person to drive up and another down. This will provide ample opportunity for sightseeing for both.

From Paulina Peak, the massive bowl that is Newberry Crater is totally visible for the first time. There are East Lake and Paulina Lake — gems of deep blue surrounded by forest green. You get a bird's eye view of the huge cinder cone separating the two lakes. Newberry's largest obsidian flow is almost directly beneath you so that you can see acres of volcanic glass.

The wind blows constantly at the summit of Paulina Peak. The misshapen and dwarfed trees bear mute testimony to its powerful force. And, even in mid-summer, it is chilly. A light jacket will feel comfortable. Perhaps the strongest emotion one gets at the summit is one of almost total detachment from the world and all its problems. This feeling makes leaving difficult. But leave one must … back down the mountainside with its spectacular view to stop at Paulina Lake Lodge.

The lodge sits at the west end of this magnificent lake which is one of Central Oregon's favorite fishing spots during the summer. A boat dock and boat launching ramp are there for the convenience of boaters and fishermen. Since Paulina Lake sits almost directly under Paulina Peak, it is virtually impossible to refrain from looking upward to its summit which you have just departed. Eagles are quite common in this area. consequently, it might be worth your while to do some of your sightseeing overhead.

The next stop after leaving Paulina Lake is the giant obsidian flow, one of the largest in the world. It is very difficult to put into words the gigantic mass of this obsidian flow. At the point of where the flow

69

stopped, it must be at least 50 feet thick. Now, if you consider that this flow had its beginning high on the caldera's rim some two miles south of the viewpoint … if you also consider that within two miles it must have filled innumerable canyons … if you realize that the flow is a mile wide … then, and only then, can you get some conception of its immensity. Its depth, at some points, must be *several hundred feet.*

East Lake affords one a better view of the caldera rim, the center cinder cone, and Paulina Peak than from any other point other than the summit of Paulina Peak. It is here that one fully realizes that he is literally "inside a volcano." It is here that one begins to comprehend the catastrophic collapse of Mt. Newberry. It is here that one becomes more aware of the awesome power of nature and creation.

The facilities at East Lake are comparable to those at Paulina Lake. A lodge and boat launching ramp are here for the public's use.

The pavement ends at Cinder Hill Campground, just north of East Lake Lodge. As a suggestion, take the loop drive through the campground, and you will be headed back past the lodge and on your way back toward Paulina Lake.

In many ways, the drive back west is more spectacular than the same drive to the east. Paulina Peak dominates the skyline. You get several good views of the big obsidian flow with Paulina Peak in the background.

As one begins the descent back toward U.S. 97 down the slopes of the once mighty Mt. Newberry, one question is inescapable — "Will it happen again?" This question has undoubtedly been asked before,

TOP: The Paulina Lake Shore Trail circles this scenic volcanic lake.
Photo by Marge Kocher

BOTTOM: A mountain biker enjoys the view of East Lake from the Crater Lake Trail.
Photo by Bob Woodward

because the Forest Service folder which you receive upon entering the caldera says:

"Since the volcanic activity in this area occurred during recent geologic time, people ask if new eruptions will take place in the near future. Newberry is considered to be a dormant volcano, not extinct. There are hot, sulfur water springs in both Paulina and East lakes. Future volcanic activity is possible. If it were to occur there would be ample forewarning."

We will take the Forest Service's word for this.

This view is from Paulina Lake Resort moorage looking east.
Photo by Geoff Hill

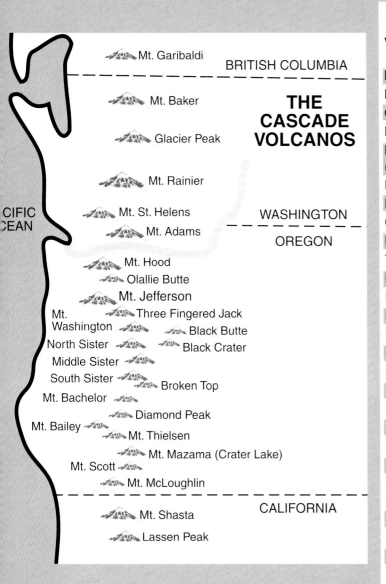

THE CASCADE VOLCANOS

VOLCANO	ELEVATION IN FEET	PROBABLE STATUS*
Mount Garibaldi	8,787	Extinct
Mount Baker	10,778	Active
Glacier Peak	10,541	Extinct
Mount Rainier	14,410	Active
Mount Saint Helens (Post Eruption 5-18-80)	9,677 / 8,500 (rim)	Active
Mount Adams	12,286	Dormant
Mount Hood	11,245	Active
Olallie Butte	7,215	
Mount Jefferson	10,495	Extinct
Three Fingered Jack	7,841	
Mount Washington	7,794	
Black Butte	6,436	
Black Crater	7,251	
North Sister	10,085	Dormant
Middle Sister	10,047	Extinct
South Sister	10,358	Active
Broken Top	9,175	
Mount Bachelor	9,065	Dormant
Diamond Peak	8,750	
Mount Thielsen	9,178	Extinct
Mount Bailey	8,363	
Mount Mazama (Crater Lake)	14,000 (est.) / 7,100 (rim)	Dormant
Mount Scott	8,926	
Mount McLoughlin	9,493	Dormant
Mount Shasta	14,161	Active
Lassen Peak	10,457	Active

*Active: The volcano presently emits steam or gas from fumaroles or vents, AND has erupted ash in recorded history.

71

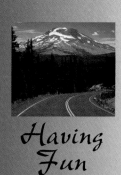

Tumalo Falls

TUMALO FALLS is one of the most striking waterfalls in the Central Oregon area, taking an almost 97-foot plunge into the rocky basin below. Located about 12 miles from Bend, there is a Forest Service day use area and a short trail to a viewpoint overlooking the falls.

A forest fire in 1979 destroyed 4,200 acres of old-growth forest in the Tumalo Falls/Tumalo Creek area and severely damaged streamside

Scars from the 1979 fire are still evident, however the falls are still an impressive sight.

The falls plunge into Tumalo Creek as seen from the lower viewpoint. Photo by Geoff Hill

habitats and wildlife cover. This devastation is still evident along the road out to the falls. Though a long way from the lush evergreen growth before the fire, the area is coming back nicely. New trees are thriving from the reforestation project with ponderosa pines done in the 80s, and fish habitat restoration work has been implemented as well.

ACTIVITIES:

BIKING: Many popular mountain bike trails may be accessed from the Tumalo Falls day-use area, including the popular North and South Fork trails. Bikers should pick up a Deschutes National Forest map to identify available trails and forest service roads accessible from this area.

CAMERA OPPORTUNITIES: Your camera is a must to capture this impressive natural wonder.

FISHING: Continuing habitat work on Tumalo Creek, which runs adjacent to the road out to the falls, has created an excellent stream for fishing. Easily accessible from the road, the creek is home to good populations of wild brook trout and rainbows. Open the entire year, fishing is restricted to artificial flies and lures only.

HIKING: A short interpretive trail leads to an overlook viewpoint above the falls. There are a number of moderate trails starting from the day-use area, including the Bridge Creek Trail and Tumalo Falls Loop Trail.

PICNICKING: Several picnic tables are located adjacent to the creek. There are vault toilets on site, however no drinking water.

AND FURTHERMORE: A Northwest Forest Pass is required to park here. The Bend Municipal Watershed is located in this area. In the winter, the falls are a popular destination for dedicated snowshoers and cross country skiers. Other ski trails are available here as well.

DIRECTIONS: *From U.S. Hwy 97 in Bend, turn west on Franklin Avenue and follow the road through downtown Bend past Drake Park to Galveston. Turn right on Galveston and follow this road (which turns into Skyliner Road) out about 11 miles to Forest Road 4601. Turn right and cross the bridge. The pavement ends but the road continues for approx. 3 miles to the Tumalo Falls Picnic Area.*

Central Oregon Directory
A List of Helpful Phone Numbers, Addresses & Web Sites

	Phone*	Address	Web Site
FOREST SERVICE OFFICES			
Bend/Fort Rock Ranger District	383-4000	1230 NE 3rd St, Suite A262; Bend, OR 97701	
Crescent Ranger District	433-3200	P.O. Box 208; Crescent, OR 97733	
Deschutes National Forest	383-5300	1645 Hwy 20E; Bend, OR 97701	www.fs.fed.us/r6/centraloregon
Sisters Ranger District	549-7700	P.O. Box 249; Sisters, OR 97759	
U.S. Forest Service			www.fs.fed.us
FOREST VISITOR CENTERS			
Lava Lands Visitor Center	593-2421	58201 S. Hwy 97; Bend, OR 97707	
Paulina Guard Station	536-8802	P.O. Box 989; Bend, OR 97709	
Mt. Bachelor Ski Area	382-2607	Cascades Lakes Hwy; Bend, OR 97702	www.mtbachelor.com
OREGON STATE OFFICES			
Oregon Department of Fish and Wildlife	388-6363	61374 Parrell Rd; Bend, OR 97702	www.df.state.or.us/
Oregon Department of Parks and Recreation	388-6211	Area 5 Office, 20300 Empire Ave., Suite B1 Bend, OR 97702	www.oregonstateparks.org
CHAMBERS OF COMMERCE			
Bend Chamber of Commerce	382-3221	777 NW Wall St., Suite 200; Bend, OR 97701	www.bendchamber.org
Bend Visitor & Convention Bureau	382-8048	63085 N. Hwy 97; Bend, OR 97701	www.visitbend.org
LaPine Chamber of Commerce	536-9771	51425 Hwy 97, Suite A, LaPine, OR 97739	www.lapine.org
Sunriver Area Chamber of Commerce	593-8149	P.O. Box 3246; Sunriver, OR 97707	www.sunriver-direct.com
RESORTS*			
Crane Prairie Resort**	383-3939	P.O. Box 1171; Bend, OR 97709	www.crane-prairie-resort-guides.com
Crescent Lake Resort	433-2505	P.O. Box 73; Crescent Lake, OR 97425	www.crescentlakeresort.com
Cultus Lake Resort**	800-616-3230	P.O. Box 262; Bend, OR 97709	www.cultuslakeresort.com
East Lake Resort**	536-2230	P.O. Box 95; LaPine, OR 97739	www.eastlakeresort.com
Elk Lake Resort	480-7248	P.O. Box 789; Bend, OR 97709	www.elklakeresort.com
Lava Lake Lodge**	382-9443	P.O. Box 989; Bend, OR 97709	
Odell Lake Resort	433-2540	P.O. Box 72: Crescent Lake, OR 97425	www.odelllakeresort.com
Paulina Lake Resort	536-2240	P.O. Box 7; LaPine, OR 97739	www.paulinalakeresort.com
Shelter Cove Resort	433-2548	P.O. Box 52; Crescent Lake, OR 97425	www.sheltercoveresort.com
Twin Lakes Resort**	593-6526	P.O. Box 3550; Sunriver, OR 97707	www.twinlakesresortoregon.com
CAMPGROUND RESERVATIONS			
Oregon State Parks Campgrounds	800-452-5687		www.oregonstateparks.org
National Forest Campgrounds	800-444-6777		www.fs.fed.us

Area Code: 541
***Summer seasonal areas*

Popular Mountain Biking Trails
A List of Some Favorite Trails

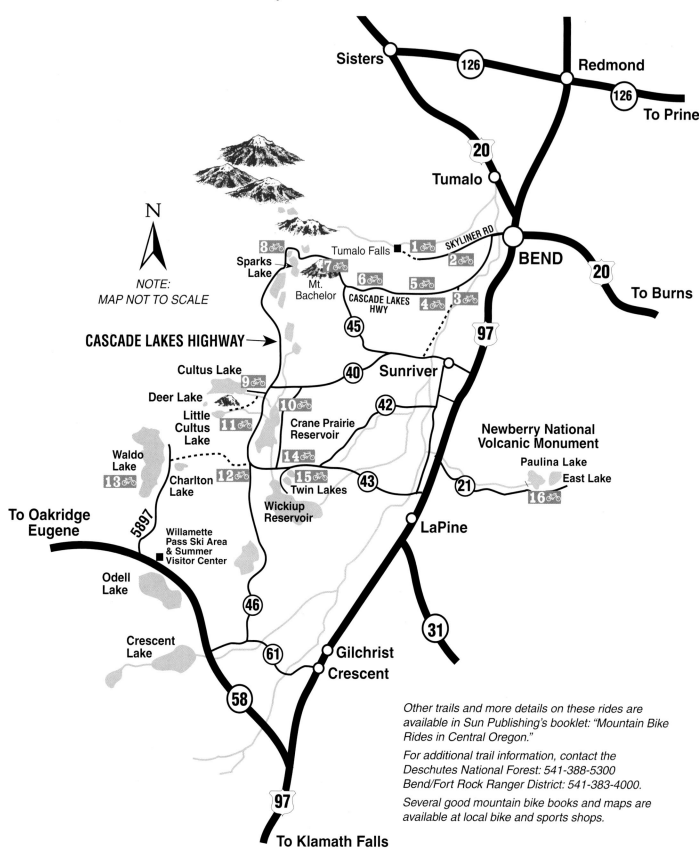

Sisters

126

Redmond

126

To Prinevi

20

Tumalo

SKYLINER RD

1

2

BEND

20

To Burns

8

Tumalo Falls

Sparks Lake

7

6

5

4

3

CASCADE LAKES HWY

Mt. Bachelor

45

97

NOTE:
MAP NOT TO SCALE

N

CASCADE LAKES HIGHWAY →

40

Sunriver

Cultus Lake

9

Deer Lake

10

Little Cultus Lake

11

42

Newberry National Volcanic Monument

Paulina Lake

East Lake

Crane Prairie Reservoir

Waldo Lake

14

13

Charlton Lake

12

15

43

21

16

Twin Lakes

Wickiup Reservoir

To Oakridge Eugene

5897

Willamette Pass Ski Area & Summer Visitor Center

LaPine

Odell Lake

46

31

Crescent Lake

61

Gilchrist

Crescent

58

Other trails and more details on these rides are available in Sun Publishing's booklet: "Mountain Bike Rides in Central Oregon."

For additional trail information, contact the Deschutes National Forest: 541-388-5300 Bend/Fort Rock Ranger District: 541-383-4000.

Several good mountain bike books and maps are available at local bike and sports shops.

97

To Klamath Falls

1

TUMALO CREEK TRAIL*

2.5 miles one way

Approx. 2 hours out and back

Easy

Summer and fall

Provides trail from Skyliner Sno-Park to Tumalo Falls

Approx. 12 miles from Bend at end of Skyliner Road; trailhead at Skyliner Sno-Park

2

PHIL'S LOOP*

13.3 miles

2 hours

More Difficult

All Seasons

A short drive from Bend, this is a locals' favorite.

Approx. 3 miles from Bend off Skyliner Road

3

INN LOOP*

13 miles roundtrip

2 hours

Easy

All Seasons

(Forest Service map helpful for this trail)

Trailhead approx. 7 miles from Bend at FS 41 off Cascade Lakes Hwy. just past The Inn of the 7th Mountain

4

KIWA BUTTE LOOP

9 miles

2 hours

Easy

Spring, Summer, Fall

Double-track loop heads downhill then gradually climbs to finish

Approx. 10 miles west of Bend off Cascade Lakes Hwy. at FS 4613 (on left side of hwy. about 3 miles past The Inn of the 7th Mountain)

5

TANGENT/ QS 1041 LOOP*

11 miles

2 hours

Easy

Spring, Summer, Fall

Rolling terrain starting at Meissner Sno-Park.

Trailhead approx. 14 miles west of Bend off Cascade Lakes Hwy. at Virginia Meissner Sno-Park; FS4615

6

SWAMPY LAKES LOOP*

4 miles

About 1 hour

Easy to Moderate

Summer, Fall

Follow the Swampy Lakes Trail from the parking lot. Numerous other trails branch off from this one for a longer trip if desired.

Trailhead approx. 16 miles west of Bend off Cascade Lakes Hwy. at Swampy Lakes Sno-Park

7

MT. BACHELOR TRAILS

Distances of trails vary

Length of time varies

Easy to More Difficult

Summer/Early Fall

Marked trails follow many of the winter cross country trails

Approx. 21 miles west of Bend off Cascade Lakes Hwy; park at the Mt. Bachelor Ski Area

8

SPARKS LAKE/LAVA LAKES*

23.5 miles

3-4 hours

More Difficult

Summer/Early Fall

Route heads south for 10 miles to Lava Lake. Return via same trail or via paved Cascade Lakes Hwy. (13.5 miles).

Trailhead approx. 25 miles from Bend off Cascade Lakes Hwy. at Sparks Lake Trail trailhead

9

CULTUS LAKE LOOP

12 miles

2-3 hours

Moderate to More Difficult

Late Spring, Summer, Fall

Starts at Cultus Lake, follows Deer Lake Trail (see #11), continues loop around north shore of Cultus Lake back to starting point.

Approx. 25 miles west of Sunriver. Park at Cultus Lake day-use picnic area parking lot

10

ROUND MOUNTAIN/LOOKOUT MOUNTAIN

23 miles

5-7 hours

More Difficult

Spring, Summer, Fall

Includes climbs up Round and Lookout mountains. Forest Service Map helpful with this ride.

Trailhead approx. 40 miles southwest of Bend at Crane Prairie Campground/Resort. Trail starts at FS 255 just outside the campground entrance

11

DEER LAKE TRAIL*

7 miles

1 hour

Easy

Late Spring, Summer, Fall

Follows north shore of Little Cultus Lake to turn-around at Deer Lake. (Take FS 640 off of Deer Lake Trail for option to climb Cultus Mountain.)

Approx. 25 miles west of Sunriver. Take FS 4636 to Little Cultus Lake; right on FS 640 to trailhead

12

CHARLTON LAKE LOOP

22 miles

5-7 hours

Strenuous

Summer, Fall

A Forest Service Map is helpful for this loop which includes several connected, marked trails

Approx. 40 miles southwest of Bend near the junction of Hwy. 42 and Hwy. 46 (Cascade Lakes Hwy.) at FS 4290

13

WALDO LAKE TRAIL*

22 miles

5-7 hours

Very Strenuous

Summer, Fall

Difficult singletrack trail with many climbs and descents. Mosquitoes love this trail in summer!

Trailhead approx. 94 miles southwest of Bend off Hwy. 58 at Waldo Lake Shadow Bay Campground

14

CRANE PRAIRIE LOOP*

10.5 miles

2-3 hours

More Difficult

Early Spring, Summer, Fall

Fairly flat but with rough roads. Views of Crane Prairie Reservoir.

Approx. 36 miles southwest of Bend off Hwy. 42 at Browns Crossing trailhead (just before the bridge over the Deschutes at FS 800)

15

TWIN LAKES TRAIL

1.2 miles one way

1 hour or less

Easy

Summer, Fall

Easy trail from North Twin Lake boat ramp to South Twin Lake Trail.

Approx. 42 miles southwest of Bend at North Twin Lake Campground.

16

CRATER RIM TRAIL*

20 miles

4-6 hours

Strenuous

Summer, Fall

Trail includes climb up Paulina Peak. Trail marked as #57.

Approx. 36 miles south of Bend in the Newberry National Volcanic Monument. Park at Paulina Falls parking lot and follow FS 21; bear right on FS 500 to Paulina Peak and Trail #57.

---

*Northwest Forest Pass required

Popular Trails for Hiking
A List of Some Favorite Trails

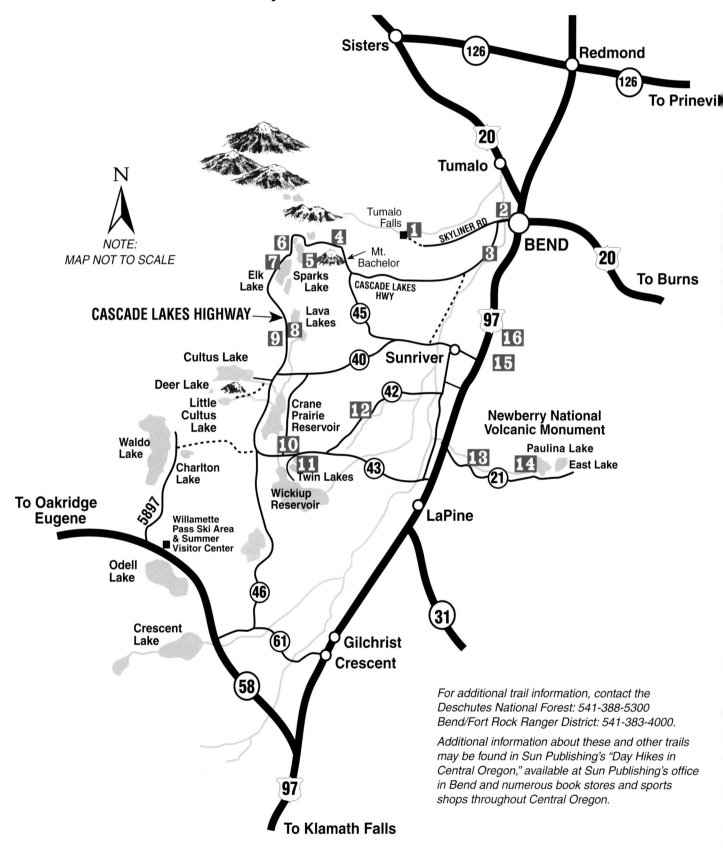

N

NOTE: MAP NOT TO SCALE

Sisters

126

Redmond

126

To Prinevil

20

Tumalo

Tumalo Falls

1

SKYLINER RD

2

BEND

3

20

To Burns

4

Mt. Bachelor

6

7

5

Elk Lake

Sparks Lake

CASCADE LAKES HWY

97

Lava Lakes

CASCADE LAKES HIGHWAY →

45

16

8

9

40

Sunriver

15

Cultus Lake

Deer Lake

Little Cultus Lake

Crane Prairie Reservoir

42

12

Newberry National Volcanic Monument

Paulina Lake

Waldo Lake

10

13

14

East Lake

Charlton Lake

11

Twin Lakes

43

21

To Oakridge Eugene

5897

Wickiup Reservoir

LaPine

Willamette Pass Ski Area & Summer Visitor Center

Odell Lake

46

31

Crescent Lake

61

Gilchrist

Crescent

58

97

To Klamath Falls

For additional trail information, contact the Deschutes National Forest: 541-388-5300 Bend/Fort Rock Ranger District: 541-383-4000.

Additional information about these and other trails may be found in Sun Publishing's "Day Hikes in Central Oregon," available at Sun Publishing's office in Bend and numerous book stores and sports shops throughout Central Oregon.

1 TUMALO FALLS LOOP*

7 miles
2-3 hours
Easy to Moderate
Summer, Fall
Approx. 15 miles west of Bend out Skyliner Rd.

Scenic loop starts near the falls and winds along several creeks

2 SHEVLIN PARK LOOP

5 miles
1-2 hours
Easy
All seasons
Approx. 4 miles west of Bend out Shevlin Park Rd.

Numerous other trails available in the park

3 UPPER DESCHUTES RIVER TRAILS*

Distance varies according to start & finish points (full length 8.5 miles one way)
Difficulty varies
Easy to moderate
Spring, Summer, Fall
Approx. 6 miles west of Bend off Century Drive at Meadow Picnic Arca

Trail follows the banks of the Deschutes River

4 TUMALO MOUNTAIN*

4-mile roundtrip
2-3 hours
Moderate to difficult
Summer, Fall
21 miles west of Bend off Century Drive at Dutchman Flat Sno-Park

Steady 2-mile climb up 7,775' Tumalo Mountain

5 RAY ATKESON LOOP TRAIL*

2.5 miles
1 hour or less
Easy
Summer, Fall
Approx. 27 miles west of Bend off Cascade Lakes Hwy. at Sparks Lake

Numerous other trails accessed from this area

6 MIRROR LAKES TRAIL*

3.5 miles one way
3-4 hours
Moderate
Summer, Fall
Approx. 30 miles west of Bend off Cascade Lakes Hwy. at Mirror Trailhead

For return, retrace trail or connect with other trails for longer loop. Wilderness Permit required (available at trailhead)

7 ELK-DEVILS TRAIL*

4.6 miles one way
3-4 hours
Moderate
Summer, Fall
Approx. 33 miles west of Bend off Cascade Lakes Hwy. right to Elk Lake Trailhead

For one-way trip, leave second car at Devils Lake. Wilderness Permit required (available at trailhead)

8 LAVA LAKE TRAIL

1.5 miles one way
1 hour
Easy
Summer, Fall
Approx. 36 miles west of Bend off Cascade Lakes Hwy. at Lava Lake Resort. Park at resort.

Trail skirts east shore of Lava Lake. Trail continues on 4.25 miles to Hosmer Lake

9 SENOJ LAKE TRAIL*

6.5 miles one way
4-5 hours
Moderate
Summer, Fall
Approx. 39 miles west of Bend off Cascade Lakes Hwy. at Lucky Lake Trailhead

Steady climb before descent to Senoj Lake. Wilderness Permit required (available at trailhead)

10 BROWNS CROSSING TRAIL*

1.6-mile roundtrip
1 hour or less
Easy
Summer, Fall
Approx. 24 miles southwest of Sunriver on FS 42 just before bridge over Deschutes at Browns Mountain Day Use parking lot

Short easy hike to Crane Prairie Reservoir dam

11 SOUTH TWIN LAKE TRAIL

1 mile loop
1 hour or less
Easy
Summer, Fall
Approx. 44 miles southwest of Bend at South Twin Campground

Short easy hike around South Twin Lake

12 FALL RIVER TRAIL*

3 miles one way or turn back at any point
Time varies according to turning point
Easy
Year-round
Approx. 40 miles south of Bend off FS 42 (Century Dr.) at Fall River Campground

Short easy hike follows the banks of Fall River

13 PAULINA CREEK TRAIL*

8.5 miles one way from Ogden Group Camp
6 miles one way from McKay Crossing
Time varies according to starting point
Moderate
Summer, Fall
Approx. 25 miles south of Bend off FS 21; follow signs to Newberry Crater

Trail follows Paulina Creek upstream to Paulina Lake past numerous waterfalls

14 PAULINA LAKE SHORE LOOP*

7-mile loop
2-3 hours
Easy to moderate
Summer, Fall
Approx. 35 miles south of Bend off FS 21; follow signs to Paulina Lake at Little Crater Campground

Trail follows the shoreline of Paulina Lake

15 LAVA CAST FOREST TRAIL*

1 mile
Less than 1 hour
Easy
Year-round weather permitting
Approx. 15 miles south of Bend off Hwy 97; turn at FS 9720 just across from Sunriver turnoff for 9 miles

Easy, paved, self-guided loop through interesting geologic formation

16 LAVA RIVER CAVE TRAIL*

1 mile
Less than 1 hour
Easy
Mid-May to mid-October
Approx. 13 miles south of Bend off Hwy 97 (about 1 mile south of Lava Lands Visitor Center)

Short trail through the largest uncollapsed lava tube in Oregon. Lanterns available for rent seasonally for a small fee

*Northwest Forest Pass required

Popular Day Use Areas
Some Favorite Spots to Relax

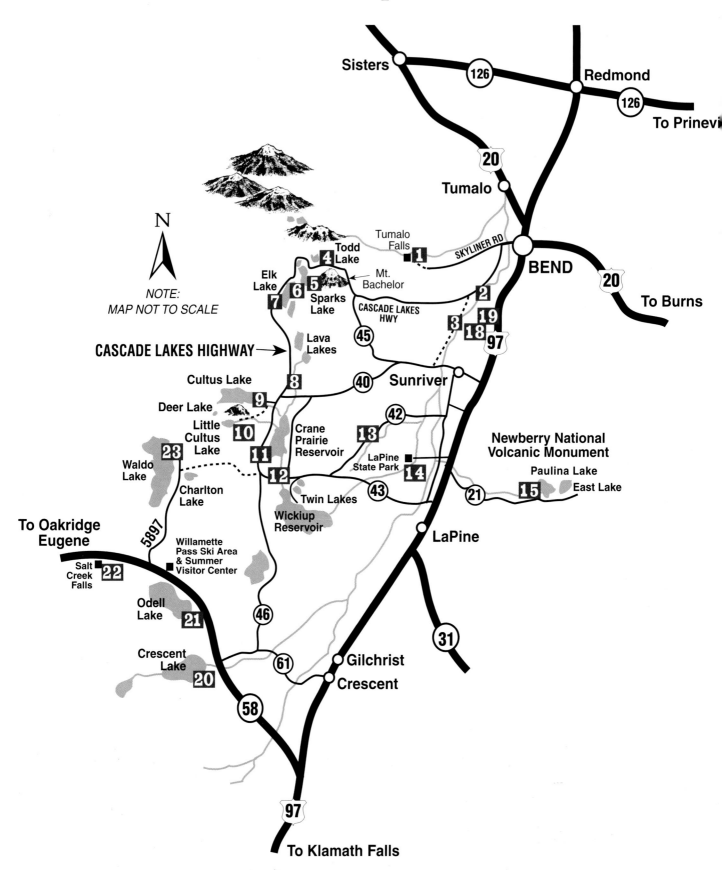

N

NOTE:
MAP NOT TO SCALE

CASCADE LAKES HIGHWAY →

Sisters

126

Redmond

126

To Prinevi

20

Tumalo

SKYLINER RD

BEND

Tumalo Falls

1

Todd Lake

4

Mt. Bachelor

Elk Lake

5

Sparks Lake

7 6

CASCADE LAKES HWY

2

20

To Burns

19

18

97

3

45

Lava Lakes

8

40

Sunriver

Cultus Lake

9

Deer Lake

42

Little Cultus Lake

10

Crane Prairie Reservoir

13

Newberry National Volcanic Monument

Paulina Lake

East Lake

23

11

LaPine State Park

14

15

Waldo Lake

12

Charlton Lake

Twin Lakes

43

21

To Oakridge Eugene

5897

Wickiup Reservoir

LaPine

Willamette Pass Ski Area & Summer Visitor Center

Salt Creek Falls

22

Odell Lake

21

46

31

Crescent Lake

20

61

Gilchrist

58

Crescent

97

To Klamath Falls

No. Day Use Area	Trailhead	Picnic	Toilets	Boat Ramp	Swimming	Fee
1. Tumalo Falls	✖	✖	✖			✖
2. Meadow Picnic Area	✖	✖	✖			✖
3. Upper Deschutes River Area	✖	✖				✖
4. Todd Lake	✖	✖	✖		✖	✖
5. Ray Atkeson Trail (Sparks Lake)	✖	✖	✖	✖	✖	✖
6. Sunset Day Use (Elk Lake)		✖	✖		✖	✖
7. Beach Day Use (Elk Lake)		✖	✖		✖	✖
8. Mile Camp Day Use		✖	✖			
9. Cultus Lake	✖	✖	✖	✖	✖	✖
10. Little Cultus Lake	✖	✖	✖	✖	✖	✖
11. Osprey Point	✖	✖	✖			✖
12. Browns Mountain Bridge	✖	✖				
13. Fall River Area	✖	✖	✖			
14. LaPine State Park	✖	✖	✖	✖	✖	
15. Paulina Falls Day Use	✖	✖	✖			✖
16. Lava Cast Forest Day Use	✖	✖	✖			✖
17. Lava River Caves Day Use	✖	✖	✖			✖
18. Benham Falls Day Use	✖	✖	✖	✖	✖	✖
19. Lava Lands Visitor Center	✖	✖	✖			✖
20. Crescent Lake Area						
Simax Beach		✖	✖		✖	
Tandy Bay		✖	✖		✖	
Tranquil Cove		✖	✖		✖	
21. Odell Lake		✖	✖	✖	✖	
22. Salt Creek Falls	✖	✖	✖			✖
23. North Waldo	✖	✖	✖	✖	✖	✖

OSPREY SANCTUARY

Crane Prairie Reservoir Osprey Management Area is a cooperative venture by the U.S. Forest Service, Bureau of Reclamation and Oregon State Game Commission to provide the Osprey, a potentially endangered species, a safe place to live and propagate.
The management area is dedicated to the protection of the Osprey and its habitat.

Two popular day use areas are Osprey Point and LaPine State Recreation area.

Left photo by Don Burgerfer
Right photo by Geoff Hill

Enjoy Our Collection of Publications

Cascades East Magazine

Enjoy interesting and informative articles season-by-season with Central Oregon's quarterly magazine since 1976.

$16.00 for one year or save and subscribe for 2 years for $28.00

FISHING Central Oregon
4th Edition

Complete Fishing Book on Central Oregon Waters!

High Quality ~180 Pages
Over 150 Bodies of Water
200 Color Photos & Maps

Just $20.00 at local merchants or at Sun Publishing's office in Bend or by mail for $23.00
(includes shipping and handling)

Freshwater Fishing
Oregon & Washington

Gary Lewis ~ Author
From Washington's Olympic Peninsula rainforests to Oregon's Outback!

High Quality ~128 Pages
In-depth Instruction
100 Color Photos

Just $18.95 at local merchants or at Sun Publishing's office in Bend or by mail for $22.00
(includes shipping and handling).

Little Known Tales from Oregon History
Volumes I, II, III, IV

Featuring more than 23 stories & over 80 photos & illustrations.
$11.95 (I, II);
$13.95 (III, IV)
at local merchants or Sun Publishing in Bend or by mail for
$15 (I, II);
$17 (III, IV)
(includes shipping & handling).

Day Hikes in Central Oregon

A collection of 18 popular day hikes in a handy pocket-size format. Hikes for all ages & abilities.

Waterfalls of Central Oregon

A collection of scenic waterfalls in Central Oregon, all within an easy drive from Bend. Includes detailed directions, maps, photos, and descriptions for each waterfall.

Mountain Bike Rides in Central Oregon

A collection of 23 rides in Central Oregon for all fitness levels with detailed directions, maps, and descriptions for each ride.

Each booklet $5.00 at Sun Publishing's office in Bend or by mail for $6.00
(includes shipping & handling).

HUNTING OREGON

Gary Lewis ~ Author
Comprehensive, 116-page hunting book covering of Oregon with over 160 photos. Year-'round opportunities.

Just $15.00 at local merchants or Sun Publishing's office in Bend or by mail for $18.00
(includes shipping & handling)